Many Happy Returns

Many Happy Returns

The Story of Henry Bloch, America's Tax Man

Thomas M. Bloch

John Wiley & Sons, Inc.

Published by John Wiley & Sons, Inc., Hoboken, New Jersey.
Published simultaneously in Canada.

For general information on our other products and services or for technical support, please contact our Customer Care Department within the United States at (800) 762-2974, outside the United States at (317) 572-3993 or fax (317) 572-4002.

Wiley also publishes its books in a variety of electronic formats. Some content that appears in print may not be available in electronic books. For more information about Wiley products, visit our web site at www.wiley.com.

Library of Congress Cataloging-in-Publication Data:

Bloch, Thomas M.
    Many happy returns : the story of Henry Bloch, America's tax man / Thomas M. Bloch.
        p. cm.
    ISBN 978-0-470-76777-1 (hardback); ISBN 978-0-470-93990-1 (ebk);
    ISBN 978-0-470-93992-5 (ebk); ISBN 978-1-118-00677-1 (ebk)
        1. Tax return preparation industry—United States.   2. Bloch, Henry W.
    3. Businesspeople—United States—Biography.   4. H & R Block.   I. Title.
    HJ2351.8.B56   2010
    338.7'6165746092—dc22
    [B]   2010021584

Printed in the United States of America

10 9 8 7 6 5 4 3 2

For Mom

Contents

Introduction by Henry W. Bloch

I never wanted a book written about me—it seemed so vain. So when a number of authors and publishers approached me over the years about writing an account of my life, I declined. But just over a year ago, at age 87, I decided that if some of my hard-won lessons could possibly benefit others, then why not share them. I also decided that if I was ever going to sum up my life, I ought to get on with it. Certainly I've had plenty of time to reach some conclusions on how it all turned out.

As a youngster, I was an average student—and believe me, I had to work hard to be average. Yet my mother instilled in me the confidence that I could do anything I put my mind to. I've not forgotten my parents. They helped shape my thinking about the future and what I could accomplish. And so did my experiences in World War II.

Most people's lives seem to turn out differently from the way they plan. Mine certainly has. When I started out, I never dreamed that H&R Block would become a household name, serving one out of seven U.S. taxpayers. When Dick and I hung our first sign outside the window of

our walk-up, second-story office at 39th and Main in Kansas City,
I never fathomed that we would someday be responsible for thousands
of tax offices in which over 500 million returns would be prepared. It
almost seems as if it were yesterday that we painted the words INCOME
TAX on two pieces of plywood on our parents' driveway.

I've often wondered why some people are lucky. Why, even when
the odds are stacked against them, do some people refuse to quit? Is it
possible to teach someone to think and act like an entrepreneur—to
create economic and social change, to shape their own destiny? This
book explores these and other questions.

Many people played a critical role in H&R Block's development.
I want to mention three. First and foremost is my brother Dick, whose
name will appear throughout this book. He was the quintessential
entrepreneur. Without him, the company would never have flourished
the way it did. Not long after the company developed a national presence,
Jerry Grossman became my right-hand man. As chief operating officer,
he served the company skillfully and faithfully. Ed Smith, our general
counsel, was much more than a lawyer. There was no one whose opinion I valued more. I miss Dick, Jerry, and Ed—and their tremendously
valuable contributions and friendship.

I am grateful to my son, Tom, who followed me as CEO of the
company, for writing this book. During our sessions together, we
reflected on the growth and development of H&R Block. I was constantly
reminded that our associates and franchisees have always been at the
core of the company's success. Our primary strength was rooted in
their entrepreneurial spirit. They did what was required—and then
some. They knew the real boss wasn't Dick or me; it was the customer.
I hope they will read this book as a tribute to their devotion and
generous contributions.

I don't believe I would have been nearly as successful without
Marion. Her love made me whole. She is a remarkable woman—
selfless and kind, beautiful and loving, gentle and strong. Although she
is in declining health, Marion continues to be the center of my life.

I make no pretense that this is a complete and definitive history
of H&R Block. Tom and I have selected the highlights—the urgent
problems, significant goals, key accomplishments, and some unforgettable

lessons. This book, which also reflects my own aspirations and philoso-phies, is as much a personal story as it is a business story.

When I retired from H&R Block 53 years after embarking on this journey with my brother, my good fortune allowed me to have something important to retire to—paying off my debt to society. I have done this primarily through philanthropy and social entrepreneurship. That hasn't been a chore; it has been a pleasure.

Since my retirement as chairman of the board in 2000, H&R Block has encountered—and in some cases has brought about—strong storms. Sitting on the sidelines, I've observed the company make missteps and, in my opinion, take too long to address them. Great companies don't put off fixing problems and learning from their mistakes. Great companies place at the center of attention understanding, anticipating, and meeting customer needs—not on satisfying short-term shareholder interests at the expense of long-term shareholder value.

I achieved much more than I ever dreamed possible. When it comes right down to it, I feel that I owe most of my success to luck. There is, I suppose, a causal relationship between good fortune and hard work. As Thomas Jefferson said, "I find the harder I work, the more luck I seem to have."

Everyone has a dream. If yours is to love what you do and to leave the world a better place, I applaud your aspiration. I encourage you to work hard—so that luck will be on your side, too.

Many happy returns.

Author's Note

As you read *Many Happy Returns*, you will come to know an unlikely American hero—a man whose ordinary, unassuming nature made him a rare corporate icon. You will view a man who never craved power or fame, though he obtained both. Henry Bloch is an illuminating example of what a person with purpose and a strong moral code can accomplish.

This is a story of how a modest, down-to-earth man created a global industry and helped millions of people. Through his philanthropy and social entrepreneurship, he enriched and helped transform his community. According to Henry, it takes hard work, a vision, and luck. In this book, he shares the secrets of his success.

You'll see the inner dynamics of H&R Block, one of the most well known brands in America. You'll learn the importance of mentoring and meet some of the people who helped shape Henry's philosophy on business and life. And you'll receive invaluable tips on entrepreneurship from the man whose name adorns one of the top schools for nascent entrepreneurs.

True success, Henry stresses, is rooted in two fundamental questions: Are you doing what you love, and are you leaving the world a better place?

Among his many qualities and accomplishments, Henry Bloch has always been a great family man. I should know—he is my father. I was born a year before the birth of H&R Block. It was 1954, one day before the tax filing deadline. While Mom was in the delivery room, Dad was in the waiting room, filling out tax forms for his bookkeeping clients.

Unbeknownst to me, my young face turned up in newspaper ads. The caption read, "Betcha MY Daddy Worries Less Than YOUR Daddy about his INCOME TAX." In third grade, I began learning about the tax business over dinner-table conversations, although I admit to having had trouble grasping what taxes were. At age 13, I swept tax office floors. Twenty-five years later, I succeeded Dad as CEO.

Having the privilege of knowing and working with my father in a most unique context gave me the opportunity to tell his story from an exceedingly close-up view. But I knew that our special relationship would create a challenge for me—to present a balanced, objective account of him, his career, and his beliefs. With the benefit of his levelheaded review of each sentence of this book along with the help of others who have known and worked with him, I hope that I succeeded.

The first of our many interviews for this book occurred in the summer of 2009. We met in his fourth floor office in midtown Kansas City. Armed with a digital recorder and a list of questions, our collaboration began. Much of the information in these pages is derived from those interviews. Although memory is not always a reliable source for a writer, it was in many instances the only source available.

Initially, I was concerned that Dad might tire of raking over his past. He is a man of action more than a man of introspection. After all, the past is over. But he was extraordinarily engaged and enthusiastic, opening up as I'd never heard him before. It was a delight sitting across his desk from him and listening to him describe his journey.

During our many one-and-a-half-hour sessions, Dad would invariably go off on tangents. It was a good thing he did. Some of the most insightful information in this book came out of those digressions. By the end of each sitting, I felt that he had taught me a lesson or two. Working on this book was a labor of love.

My final interview with Dad occurred on a Saturday morning at his home. I let myself into the house and proceeded up the back stairway to my parents' bedroom. I found my ailing mother asleep in her recliner chair. My father sat in a chair by her side. "I just love to hold her hand," he said to me as I walked into the room.

"Henry is the best that human nature has to offer," one of his closest friends told me. Block associates describe him as approachable, humble, good-humored, honest, and infallibly polite. His family portrays him as a devoted husband and loving father.

The average tenure of a CEO at this time is about five years—but Henry was at the helm for five *decades*. Even more remarkable is that, despite a daily buffeting of reality, his idealism and drive never diminished.

Any profits I receive from this book will be used to support the Henry W. Bloch School of Business and Public Administration at the University of Missouri-Kansas City. Henry has been intimately involved in supporting and guiding the school for nearly 25 years. The Bloch School, which houses the esteemed Institute for Entrepreneurship and Innovation, is ranked by the Princeton Review among the top 25 graduate entrepreneurship programs in the United States.

In an era rife with corruption and greed, Henry Bloch inspires us to work hard, be honest, and follow our dreams. His example of American ingenuity and values had an unprecedented effect on how I, along with countless others who have known and worked beside him, view the world. I welcome your reactions. You can reach me at www.henrybloch.com.

Many Happy Returns

Chapter 1

A Chip Off the Ol' Block

Henry Bloch sat on the edge of his seat in the darkened movie theater. Though he had seen many films in his 13 years, this story of Louis Pasteur inspired him in a new way. He admired how Pasteur had saved thousands of lives and made a difference in the world. And sitting there in Kansas City, he knew he too wanted to make such a difference. But he had no idea how he would do it.

"Go into business with your brothers," his mother always said. Henry tried to listen to his mother. She was a woman passionate about her sons, her husband and Ralph Waldo Emerson. She believed in thinking for herself, and she tried to teach her sons the same. "Don't go where the path may lead, go instead where there is no path and leave a trail," his mother told him, quoting Ralph Waldo Emerson.

She looked at Henry and saw his potential to start a new path. But in the 1930s most people would not have looked at the shy and wiry Henry and seen a world-changing kid. In school his teachers labeled him as average, and even he admitted his brothers were smarter.

Born in 1922, Henry Bloch was the middle son of a middle-class family smack in the middle of the country. He was a conscientious, hardworking student, even though his grades put him in the middle of his class.

"Math was the only subject I was good at," he acknowledges. "I couldn't do foreign languages. I flunked French and German in high school." Besides math, he was interested in science, though his grades didn't always reflect his eagerness to master the subject.

Henry might say that his parents, Leon and Hortense, proved a scientific law: opposites attract. Leon had a voracious appetite for travel. Horty, as she was better known, was a consummate homebody. He was frugal and she enjoyed spending. Both were raised Jewish, but only Leon practiced the faith. Horty said, "I believe in Emerson," a devotion made apparent by the collections of Emerson's essays, journals, and poems in her sitting room.

Among the countless Emerson maxims that Horty quoted, one in particular stuck with Henry: "Every institution is the lengthened shadow of one man." Little did he know when his mother uttered these words that they would become intensely appropriate to him.

Horty and Leon may have been opposites, but both of them enjoyed card games. "My parents played lots of bridge with their friends," Henry recollects. "The only time I ever heard them come close to having an argument was over a card game. Dad would say, 'Horty, Horty, how could you do that!' "

But Leon never let an imperfect bridge game stand in the way of a near-perfect marriage. In a 1945 letter to his sweetheart, Leon wrote, "Started to figure just how many times my love for you has increased and how precious you have become, but failed to find the figure."

Horty and Leon had three children. Leon Jr. was the oldest. Henry was born two years later, the middle son. Richard, better known as "Dick," was born more than three years after Henry. Horty named her second son after her beloved uncle Henry Wollman, a promi-nent New York attorney. Aside from occasional spats, the three Bloch

Henry's parents, Hortense (Horty) and Leon

brothers benefited throughout their youth from a remarkably close relationship.

Leon Sr. was a fair but strict father. Horty was an easygoing and tolerant mother. "Mom tried to spoil her children," Henry says. "It was not unusual for her to slip us extra spending money."

"Don't tell Dad," she always counseled. It was a good thing she was generous because the boys never received an allowance.

Henry remembers his father as an authoritarian figure. "When it was time for dinner, he'd come to my room and say, 'Come downstairs.' Then he would turn out my light and walk out. No matter what I was doing, I was expected to follow right behind him."

Leon Jr. says, "If we failed to mind Father, we'd definitely regret it."

Childhood Lessons

With three boys who could each show a mischievous streak, it was a good thing that their father was firm. Once Leon Jr. chased Henry around the breakfast room table. Henry ran past his dad's tool drawer and grabbed a small handsaw with a pointed blade. He threw it over his shoulder and the blade went through Leon's nose. Now, at age 89, Leon still exhibits a scar as a reminder of that childhood incident.

But turnabout is fair play. "Once I got locked out on the second-floor porch by one of my brothers," Henry explains. "I used my fist and broke the window to get back in." He too displays a permanent mark.

The three boys loved to scale the massive chestnut trees in the vacant lot next door. Sometimes they dislodged the prickly chestnuts, and other times they climbed in the house through a second-story window. Their mother often warned them, illogically, "If you fall and break both legs, don't come running home to me."

Henry had an insatiable curiosity. "I had a chemistry set when I was a kid, and I figured out how to make ammonia. I showed the flask to Mom, and I told her to smell. She collapsed. Dick yelled, 'You killed my mother!'"

The Bloch brothers (left to right): Richard, Henry, and Leon

The ammonia didn't kill her, nor did endless cross-country road trips with her husband and three sons. On their first such trip, the five Blochs drove to California. Henry was thrilled to see the Grand Canyon and the Pacific Ocean. The vacation, as it turned out, was more eventful than any of them could have imagined. They got a flat tire in the middle of nowhere. "We determined that a filling station owner had sprinkled tacks on the highway. Like other victims, we were stuck paying him to patch the tire," Henry recalls. That wasn't the only mishap.

It was a hot day in the California desert, and cars didn't yet have air conditioning. "We kept a thermos in our car. Mom filled the top full of water and handed it to Dad, who was driving. After taking a sip, he threw what was left out the window. But he had forgotten to open the window and the water splashed back on him."

In a nondescript town in the Nevada desert, the family stopped at a roadside cafe. Horty recognized Herbert Hoover sitting at the next table. A courageous Henry asked the former president for his autograph and Hoover complied by writing it on a guest check.

Henry always enjoyed family vacations. Once, though, he convinced the family to cut short their travels. They had driven to the 1933 World's Fair in Chicago. Eleven-year-old Henry, who was keen on going to the movies, was eager to see a highly anticipated adventure film. *Tarzan the Fearless*, starring the athletic Buster Crabbe and the popular Jacqueline Wells, was to be released in Kansas City before their scheduled return. The family consented to come home early so Henry could watch the amazing Tarzan and his companion Mary (instead of Jane) swing through the trees.

The Tarzan series was among Henry's favorites. Other than *The Story of Louis Pasteur*, though, nothing Henry absorbed from the surreal world of the silver screen could touch the long-lasting impact made by some real-life incidents of his youth.

"I was maybe 12 years old and home alone when the doorbell rang. A salesman was pushing magazine subscriptions. I ran up to my room where I kept a few dollars. I paid him five dollars for a one-year subscription to *Spur*, a magazine in which I had absolutely no interest. After shutting the door, I thought to myself, 'What have I done?' I was awfully disappointed in myself. When my mother came home, I told her about my blunder. I thought she would be furious. 'Wonderful!' she said. 'You'll never make that mistake again.'" Thriftiness would become a hallmark of Henry's style throughout his long business career.

Henry made a different mistake the day his namesake, his great-uncle Henry Wollman, died. The 13-year-old had recently taken up golf and was particularly fond of the sport. A fierce competitor who loved to win, Henry worked hard to hone his game. "It was Friday the 13th. I was in the front yard chipping golf balls over my parents' car. One ball went right through our dining room window." Henry braced himself as his mother opened the front door, her face awash with grief. But suddenly he felt a different kind of anguish when she broke the news of Henry Wollman's death.

Henry Wollman was a big man with a big personality. He loved a fine cigar, even if the ashes frequently landed on his large stomach. Having never married, he took an immense interest in his nieces and nephews. He always brought them a dollar, although he would first pretend to have no money. Young Henry didn't know his great-uncle well, but he always enjoyed hearing his mother's stories about Henry Wollman's warmth, his concern for family, and his significant philanthropy. In so many ways, Henry Wollman Bloch would take after Uncle Henry Wollman.

At age 15, Henry Bloch ventured to Colorado on his first trip without the family. He and his pal Maynard Brown caught a ride with friends of their parents, who were heading to California on vacation. The boys decided to hitchhike back to Kansas City, a common form of travel in the 1930s. A pleasant-enough stranger picked them up, but he had clearly been drinking. Henry asked the drunk driver to drop them off at the next town. Standing on an empty street corner late at night in Manhattan, Kansas, the boys realized that they wouldn't be able to find another ride until morning. Worse, after turning their pockets inside out, they discovered there wasn't enough money between them for a motel room.

They remembered passing a field with haystacks just before entering the town. Surely the hay would make a satisfactory mattress for one night. But getting to that field on foot took considerably longer than they thought. They were bushed when they got there. "We climbed on a haystack, determined to use it as a bed," Henry recalls. "The problem was that we couldn't get comfortable and the haystacks smelled awful. We slid down and walked aimlessly back into town. A police officer stopped us, thinking we were vagrants." The officer wasn't angry with the boys. In fact, he did them a favor by locking them up for the night. At least the jail cots smelled a bit better than the haystacks.

Early the next morning, a still-weary Henry noticed signatures of past prisoners scribbled on the cell walls. With nothing else to do, he innocently added his own autograph to the collection. "You shouldn't have done that," an inmate in the adjacent cell cautioned. "It means you'll be back."

Those words were forever etched in the teenager's mind. "Since then," Henry admits, "I've always been extremely careful to do the right thing."

The following summer, Henry decided that earning money was the right thing to do. He looked for physical work, hoping to add muscle on his lean frame. Searching the classified ads, he landed a position with the city as a ditch digger. Entirely unimpressed with her son's career choice, his mother, perhaps intentionally, forgot to wake him up on the first day. Having lost his job before he had started, Henry didn't dig a single hole.

Determined to find another job, Henry saw an ad for a grain tester. (Kansas City has long been one of the largest rail hubs and agribusiness centers in the country.) But that job didn't work out much better. "It was so dusty inside those cars, you could hardly breathe," he recalls. Henry could hardly wait to quit. From that short and unsatisfying summer experience, Henry learned about the kind of job he *didn't* want to make into a career. Sitting behind a desk seemed much more appealing.

Without a Road Map

Throughout high school Henry had no definite idea about what he wanted to study in college. "I often rode my bike to Loose Park, sat on a hill overlooking the pond, and asked myself what I wanted to do. My father told me he did the same thing when he grew up in Minneapolis, Kansas," Henry says. "I knew I wanted more than a job. I wanted to contribute something to society."

Meanwhile, an uncommon entrepreneurial curiosity overtook one of his brothers. "Dick was always a businessman," Henry says, "even as a kid." Rummaging through an uncle's attic at age four, Dick had stumbled on an old hand-powered printing press, which he found fascinating. In high school, he ran a genuine printing business with three automatic presses on the second floor of the family home. "Mother would have a mahjong game," Henry remembers, "and Dick would solicit stationery orders from the women." But his primary market was serving the printing needs of area schools. Although the business was a small moneymaker, there was a downside. Every time Dick turned on one of the presses, the house shook as if it was at the epicenter of an earthquake. When he finally sold the thunderous machines to a small college in Iowa, the family rejoiced over the renewed tranquility of their home.

In another of a string of entrepreneurial pursuits, Dick converted the family's front yard into a used car lot. He would buy malfunctioning cars, fix them, and then put them up for sale. Once again he produced a profit, which he used to defray his college expenses.

Dick pursued entrepreneurial activities the way other students engaged in sports and other extracurricular diversions. He didn't hit the books as hard as his two brothers, but he managed to make high marks. He also managed to skip school—with parental permission and without sacrificing his educational footing. Whenever Leon Sr. asked his sons if they wanted to take a trip with him during the school year, Dick was usually the only volunteer. While his brothers were hunched over their textbooks, Dick was beginning to envision a career that entailed extensive travel.

Not interested in going away to school at age 16, Henry attended the University of Kansas City. Early in his first semester he decided to become a chemist. (After all, he knew how to make ammonia.) Art, a friend from high school, also attended UKC and wanted to be a chemist. "He was brilliant," Henry recalls. "We took the same courses, and his grades were always better. But once I somehow got a B on a paper and Art got a C. He went straight to the professor. 'How could you give Henry Bloch a better grade than you gave me?' By the end of the semester, I had given up on becoming a chemist because I couldn't keep up with Art."

After freshman year, Henry was ready to venture away from Kansas City. Settling on the University of Michigan was an easy decision because his great-aunt Kate Wollman offered to pay his tuition. She made good on her brother Henry Wollman's promise to pay for his grandnieces' and grandnephews' college education at his alma mater. Only Henry and two of his cousins accepted her generous offer. Leon Jr. attended the University of Missouri. Dick set off for the Wharton School of Finance at the University of Pennsylvania, and his parents paid his way.

At the University of Michigan, Henry majored in mathematics. "It was the only subject that mattered to me," he says. "Sometimes I would sit up all night trying to work problems." He was so skillful at solving complex equations that when one of his math professors needed a substitute instructor, he figured Henry should be his replacement.

Henry thought about becoming a math teacher himself. But his mother wasn't fond of the idea. "Our family doesn't have ambition," she told him, noting that her husband, a self-employed lawyer, never aspired to have a highly successful and prosperous career. "I hope you do. And I hope you'll go into business with your brothers."

For the moment, Henry was making a small business out of playing bridge at Michigan. Like his parents and brothers, he was passionate about the game. "There was a regular match at midnight in my dorm," Henry recalls. "My roommate agreed to pay all of my losings for half of my winnings. The only problem was that I couldn't sleep afterwards. One hand after another would go through my mind."

Without a roadmap for the future in mind, Henry embarked on his last year of college. It was 1942 and the world was in turmoil. Adolph Hitler had invaded Poland, war had broken out throughout Europe, and the horrific conflict had become global. Dark and grim days lay ahead. But as Oscar Wilde once said, "What seems to us as bitter trials are often blessings in disguise." Henry's life was about to change during the bitter trial of World War II. It would shape the rest of his days.

HENRY'S DEDUCTIONS

- Don't settle for a job. Find your calling and follow your heart.
- Keep growing, learning, and changing. There's always room for improvement.
- Don't do anything that wouldn't make your parents proud.

Chapter 2

Heaven Can Wait

The card players sat quietly at their tables, thoughtfully going about their matches. Henry analyzed his hand and looked at his partner and friend, Jim Helzberg. They were in the middle of a campuswide bridge tournament, and Henry was hoping to make a good showing. As he lay down a card, a student burst into the room, shouting, "The Japanese attacked Pearl Harbor!"

Henry dropped his cards and looked at Jim. All around him, people were crying and shouting. Henry raced out of the room, searching for a radio to hear the news firsthand. The following day he listened intently as Roosevelt declared war on Japan. As the conflict escalated, some of Henry's fraternity brothers signed up or were drafted. Henry also felt an obligation to serve his country.

"JOIN THE ARMY AIR CORPS!"

The headline of the ad caught Henry's attention in the fall of 1942. He had begun his senior year at the University of Michigan. The world had drastically changed since Pearl Harbor, and there was a critical need for aircrews. He phoned the number in the ad for more information.

"If you sign up now, you can finish college before being called to serve," the recruiter assured him. That sealed the deal.

"I wanted to be a part of the war," Henry explains. "I knew it was the right thing to do." Henry also knew he wanted to be an airman. Living in a trench and engaging the enemy face-to-face appealed to him less than fighting in the air. "I understood it would be dangerous, but I wanted to fly."

After Henry enlisted, Uncle Sam changed his mind. American casualties were heavier than expected and Henry was called up at the beginning of his last semester.

George Washington said, "There is nothing so likely to produce peace as to be well prepared to meet the enemy." But 20-year-olds like Henry were hardly prepared to meet the enemy. That's why he and thousands of other college students were in line for a different kind of education.

At the San Antonio Aviation Cadet Center, better known as SAACC and pronounced "sack," new recruits received rigorous physical training and testing. As Henry earned credits at his new school, his father focused on getting him credits from his old school. In a letter to the University of Michigan, Leon made a convincing case that Henry deserved a diploma. His son was so close to graduating and would have surely fulfilled his final requirements if it weren't for an early call to defend his country.

While awaiting a response, Leon and Horty received an unexpected letter from the head of SAACC. Major General Brant wrote, "In a memorandum which has come to my desk this morning, I note that your boy, now an Aviation Cadet, has been specially selected for training as a Pilot in the Army Air Forces. . . . Men who will make good material for training as Pilots are rare. . . . I congratulate you and him."

A proud Henry phoned his parents from San Antonio, excited about becoming a pilot. His mother was furious. "If you become a pilot, your father is going to Washington, D.C., to get you out of the service," she told him. She insisted he select a safer position on the plane. Despite failing to find logic in her argument, Henry listened to his mother.

"I chose to become a navigator," Henry says. "Mom didn't really know what it was, but in her mind it wasn't as dangerous as being a pilot."

The second stop for the pilot-turned-navigator-in-training was HAGS, the Harlingen (Texas) Army Gunnery School. There he practiced sighting, swinging, and shooting the twin .50 caliber machine guns mounted on a B-17 bomber. After passing the gunnery exam with the highest possible score, he was off to navigation school at the Army Air Field in Hondo, Texas. Here he learned how to make instrument readings in flight, when to give position reports, how to keep a log, and how to use dead reckoning, which determines a plane's position in flight. He was also taught how to bail out of the plane in case of emergency. Henry quizzed the instructor, asking why trainees didn't actually practice parachuting out of a plane. He couldn't argue with the answer: "You have to do it right the first time."

The final chapter of Henry's training occurred at MacDill Air Base in Tampa, where he learned the ins and outs of the B-17, commonly called the Flying Fortress. The Flying Fortress was a long-ranging, four-engine plane stuffed with ten men, nine machine guns, and up to 4,000 pounds of bombs. It had a reputation for being able to absorb a brutal pounding from German fighters and artillery.

Henry's training left a lasting impression on him. "The Army can be the way you make it, and I must confess that, with the exception of getting up at 5 A.M., I honestly think it's the greatest place in the world except home," Henry wrote his mother. "I made up my mind that when I got here I was going to be right 'on the ball' and I have been. Doing everything the best I could and working till I was exhausted and cursing the officers—and it paid. Now my record is spotless and my conscience free. I have been given many responsibilities in the training of others, making the future look bright. . . . Don't think that I have grown conceited or such because I haven't—I am only trying to tell you how the Army appeals to me and how I believe a soldier should act."

Off to War

After a year of comprehensive training, Lieutenant Henry Bloch stood in New York Harbor sporting his second-class officer wings. Along with several thousand men in uniform, he prepared to ship out on the largest ship in the world, the RMS *Queen Elizabeth*. It had been transformed into a grey-painted troopship to transport hundreds of thousands of servicemen. Instead of spacious staterooms, they would be jam-packed into unadorned cabins furnished with wooden bunkbeds.

As he boarded the *Elizabeth*, Henry understood there would be no more dress rehearsals. But he wasn't afraid. "I knew this war was worth fighting," he says. "I wasn't thinking about myself." He was thinking about his mother.

"She was not in good health," Henry recalls. Maybe it was from the stress of seeing two of her three children go to war. Leon Jr. was drafted and sent to Hawaii when he was halfway through law school. Then Henry enlisted. (Dick was too young to serve in the military.) "Dad instructed me not to tell her I was going to fly in combat. So I told her I was doing navigation training." None of Henry's letters would mention a word about combat.

A member of the 95th Bomb Group of the 8th Air Force, Henry arrived at Horham Airfield in eastern England. An escort ushered him to a Nissen hut, a tunnel-shaped corrugated steel building in which the men slept. Bunks lined the sides of the dimly lit space.

"This is your bunk," Henry's escort announced, gesturing to a bunk that had someone else's belongings on it. A soldier jumped off a nearby bunk and hastily swept the items off the bunk and into a sack.

Lieutenant Henry Bloch

"The man who slept here last night was shot down today," the soldier said matter-of-factly. Henry bowed his head, squared his shoulders, set down his duffel, and began making his bed.

He met the other nine members of his B-17 crew, including commanding pilot Frank Psota, formerly a student and campus policeman at the University of Chicago. A month prior to joining the Air Corps, Frank got married. "Before shipping out, his wife gave him a stick of her lipstick for good luck," Henry recalls. "He rubbed it on the back of his hand before each mission." Henry had neither a wife nor a good-luck charm.

He toured the airfield and familiarized himself with all the aircraft. Each of the Flying Fortresses had a moniker painted on its side. There were names like *Lucky Strike*, *Dry Martini*, *Wham Bam*, *Yankee Doodle*, and *She's a Honey*. Henry and Frank flew most of their missions on *Heaven Can Wait*. She had a good name but had certainly seen better days.

The next morning at the crack of dawn, Henry and the other navigators attended a briefing at which they received instructions on the day's target and flight plan. Meanwhile, Frank and the rest of *Heaven Can Wait*'s crew, all of whom were Catholic, conducted their own meeting of sorts. "We prayed, we crossed, we did everything," Frank, now a retired dental surgeon, said. "We prayed also for the people that were down there [on the ground]. Some of the things we dropped were horrific."[1]

The Royal Air Force flew its missions in the dark of night, and the U.S. Air Corps made its precision-bombing attacks during the day. Berlin, the Germans' nerve center, stood as the strategic focus of a daunting first mission for Henry. The Nazis defended no target better than their capital. On a beautiful spring morning in April 1944, *Heaven Can Wait* was among hundreds of Flying Fortresses that took off, each with a full bomb load. Flying in a tight formation, the B-17s were escorted by fighter planes charged with protecting the bombers against German fighters. The air turbulence, caused by the crisscrossing wakes of so many aircraft moving together in flight, was relentless. Although Henry managed to cope with the extreme choppiness, he wondered how the airmen who had gotten dreadfully seasick on the *Elizabeth* could tolerate the bumpy mission. At an altitude of 10,000 feet, he slipped on his oxygen mask.

German fighter planes approached as the B-17s crossed into hostile airspace. From the window next to Henry's seat, he caught glimpses of the clashes between swerving U.S. and German fighters. It was like a movie, Henry thought, except this was real. "Some of our bombers fell out of formation," Henry recalls. "They were easy prey for the Germans." *Heaven Can Wait* remained in formation, continuing deeper over enemy territory.

Ten minutes before reaching a target, U.S. fighter planes were always instructed to turn back, leaving the bombers less protected as they pressed on toward Berlin. "The skies filled with flak," Henry says, describing the bursting shells of antiaircraft fire directed from the ground. "We were hit multiple times. Every hit was swift and sharp, tearing through the plane's skin." He could smell the exploding shards of hot metal through his oxygen mask. "I wondered how many blows our plane could take."

In the final minutes before arriving at the target, B-17s were not allowed to take evasive action, even with a high concentration of enemy fire. "We were ordered to go to the target at any cost," Henry says. "As soon as the leader dropped its bombs, we did the same."

Due to the intensity of artillery fire, *Heaven Can Wait* lost three of her four engines as she let her bombs fall. The plane rapidly lost altitude. Somehow, the crew got her under control and kept her steady during the prolonged and grim return trip, barely making it back to Horham.

"During my tour of duty as a navigator, I never felt more useful than on that first mission," Henry recalls. "Our plane was out of fuel when we landed, and I was completely wiped out."

At the base, it was customary for the men to drink whiskey after a successful mission. "More often than not, I preferred a game of cards over a drink," Henry says. But this was a special celebration because they were only the second group to have successfully raided Berlin. Henry raised a glass to his crew members, wondering what destiny had in store for him.

"The war taught me to be a fatalist," he says. "I never knew what the next day would bring. But I figured I had a job to do, and I would give it my all."

With fellow fatalist Eleanor Roosevelt, he agreed: "You have to accept whatever comes and the only important thing is that you meet it with courage and with the best that you can give."

Henry and his fellow airmen took part in some of the war's most intensive bombing campaigns against German targets. They hit ammunition plants, bridges, factories, and oil fields. A typical mission lasted 10 or 11 hours, involving hundreds of B-17s flying in formation. "Our battered plane had to be patched up after each mission," Henry says. After a few laudable missions, he received a performance evaluation and an early promotion, collecting his first-class officer wings.

On one of Henry's missions, his plane zigzagged down the runway on takeoff—with a full bomb load. "Finally, at the last minute, we got her up," Henry recalls. Another time he rose from his seat while in flight to determine if the bombs were hitting the target. Then came a blast. "When I turned around, a portion of one side of our plane— the side where I had been sitting—was gone." Gazing at the punched hole, Henry felt simultaneous relief and horror. The crew struggled to control their damaged plane. Remarkably, no one was wounded, and the crater didn't force them down.

Henry (first row, far left) and the other officers of *Heaven Can Wait's* bomber crew

"I'll never forget when we were over the North Sea," Henry says, describing a later mission. "German fighter planes were attacking. I looked out the window and saw the plane next to us get hit. An airman jumped out. Then, one by one, the rest of the crew followed just before the plane went down. Cold sweat ran down my back. You can't live long in that freezing water, and there was nothing I could do to help them."

Frank remembers their strike on a ball-bearing plant in Schweinfurt. "The entire German air force met us there, and I saw the biggest dog-fights of my life. We lost close to 60 airplanes total, including Fortresses and Fighters. . . . We got the heck shot out of us. [But] we destroyed the plant."[2]

Halfway through his tour of duty, on June 6, 1944, better known as D-Day, Henry flew three missions. "We had known that a major military operation was imminent," he says, "but we didn't know exactly when the assault would start. It was a battle we were eager for." A staggering 160,000 Allied troops landed that day on the coast of Normandy, which had been occupied by the Nazis. The invasion at Omaha Beach involved 5,000 ships and 13,000 aircraft. The crew of *Heaven Can Wait* was ordered to "soften up" the beach for the arriving troops. Although each of his three missions that day lasted only about one hour, Henry knew they were an important part of the seaborne invasion. The bombers provided protection for the approaching infantrymen, who faced concentrated firepower from enemy positions on the beach.

A tour of duty for navigators was initially 25 missions. But as the rate of casualties increased, the threshold was raised to 30. Though Henry had looked forward to ending his tour, he wasn't troubled by the increase in missions. "When I reached 31 missions, I was given a choice between staying for another tour or returning to the homeland. I figured I had been lucky enough." Henry sent a telegram home, not to his parents but to Scrappy, the family's beloved dog! "MISSIONS COMPLETE. ON MY WAY HOME."

A Lucky Bastard

Every airman who completed his tour of duty at Horham was inducted into The Lucky Bastards Club. There wasn't an actual ceremony because the Club had no officers. Membership was automatic and free. It involved no medals, privileges, or responsibilities. But Henry felt fortunate to become affiliated with such an elite group. He was even more delighted to receive a different honor at Horham: his diploma from the University of Michigan.

On September 5, 1944, in Gourock, Scotland, Henry boarded the RMS *Queen Mary*, also known as the *Grey Ghost*. Only 1,000 men were allowed on this crossing because a rather prominent passenger—Winston Churchill—was expected on board. (World heavyweight boxing champion Joe Louis, the "Brown Bomber," was also on the ship.) An entire deck was assigned to the prime minister and his entourage. He was destined for Quebec via Halifax for a meeting with President Roosevelt.

"Our departure was delayed one week as we waited for Churchill," Henry recalls. "It was unfortunate because there were wounded soldiers on board, some of whom did not survive the holdup." Once Churchill finally embarked, the ship departed for Halifax with an armada for escort. "To avoid submarines, the ship took evasive action by zigzagging across the Atlantic."

One day Frank got lost on the colossal ship. "I was walking in a hallway where the carpet was up to my knees, and I figured I was in the wrong place. I passed a room and I looked in, and there he was in his black jacket with cigar." It was Churchill, of course. "Charming man. My hero. I saluted him and said, 'Sir, how do I get out of here without getting shot?'"[3]

While Frank strolled in a restricted area, Henry hunted for a card game. He found one—unfortunately. "I started with less than a hundred dollars. It was everything I had. And I lost all of it." He was stuck with reading a book for entertainment during the balance of the crisscrossing passage.

Though he was a loser at the poker table, Henry came out a winner in the war game. To have flown 31 combat missions was a notable feat. In fact, the statistics indicate that an airman in the 8th Air Force had only a one-third chance of surviving his tour of duty. Summing up his war experience, Henry says, "It was no bed of roses." But at least heaven did indeed wait for him.

After dropping off Churchill in Halifax, the RMS *Queen Mary* headed for New York Harbor. Twenty-two-year-old Henry had endured and accomplished much in the previous two years. He had earned the Air Medal and three Oak Leaf Clusters for meritorious service. His unit received a Presidential Citation for extraordinary heroism in action against an armed enemy. But the Air Corps wasn't finished with Henry.

After taking leave in Kansas City to visit his parents and his dog, he reported for his next compulsory assignment. The Army had set up a special program in conjunction with Harvard Business School to train officers in statistical control. A set of highly selective admissions criteria was developed to determine which men to place in the program. Henry was among the high fliers who were picked.

At Harvard, life began to return to normal. Instead of living day to day as he did while fighting overseas, he started feeling confident about the future and his ability to succeed. A series of flawless combat missions gave him a higher sense of self-assurance. So did his selection in the exclusive Army Air Corps' officer-training program. Though he was poised to take on a different kind of mission in a postwar world, he still didn't know what career path to pursue after his stint in the service. Often he skipped lunch, browsing the bookshelves of the library for inspiration. One day, he stumbled on a pamphlet that gave him an idea.

HENRY'S DEDUCTIONS

- Don't worry about things you can't control—it's a waste of time.
- Meet adversity with courage.
- The difference between success and failure is usually in the little things.

Chapter 3

Three Nobodies
with an Idea

"What were the odds that I'd ever have an opportunity to study at Harvard?" Henry, a self-described average student, asks. "It was an experience I've always treasured." At the Army Air Corps' officer training program at Harvard Business School, First Lieutenant Henry Bloch lived in Dunster House, a red-brick dormitory on the banks of the Charles River. His life as a student on one of the world's most classically elegant and intellectually engaging college campuses stood in direct contrast with his time as a bombardier residing in a prefabricated steel hut.

During the fall of 1944, Henry wrote lengthy letters from a desk in his small dorm room to Dick, who was a college senior in Philadelphia, and to Leon Jr., who was stationed in Hawaii. Henry's correspondence reveals an optimistic and ambitious young man:

> I used to think that in the Army I was just marking time,
> but I don't anymore. I'm really getting much more done now

than I could if I were in civilian life. Occasionally I spend my nights . . . reading books and making notes.

Another letter offers a glimpse of a typical day:

I am in class from 8 to 5 every day with 3 or 4 hours of home-work each night, but I manage to spend an hour or two reading books on corporations every day. I find that I enjoy it as much as a date or a show—in fact I haven't seen a picture show in over 2 months.

To soak up as much knowledge as possible, he often went to Baker Library at the Harvard Business School. Baker, with its typical musty library smell, was anything but a typical library. Its massive stacks of manuscripts and books about business and economics spanning seven centuries were overwhelming. On one occasion a 16-page booklet entitled "Enterprise in Postwar America" drew Henry's attention. It was the transcript of a speech delivered in January 1943 by Sumner H. Slichter, a Harvard professor and one of the most highly respected economists of his day. As Henry browsed through the pages, ideas and information swirled in his mind. He needed to check out the booklet and study its every word that evening.

Slichter spoke of a transition from a war economy to a "catching-up" economy. He predicted that in peacetime new businesses would spring up, opening up exceptional opportunities for investors to fund start-ups. "Up to the present," Slichter noted, "investment companies have played only a small role in supplying capital to concerns which are about to be born."[1] He pointed out the danger in going down this road. "One must consider the risks of backing new ventures. The majority of new concerns fail."[2]

Having beaten the most daunting of odds by surviving his air com-bat missions, Henry was not deterred by the risks of starting a business. He immediately began to picture himself and his two brothers back in Kansas City operating an investment firm to support budding busi-nesses in the postwar "catching-up" economy.

Buoyed by Professor Slichter's work and anxious to share his remark-able insights, Henry wasted no time composing a letter late that night to his brothers. On his way to class the next morning, he inserted the

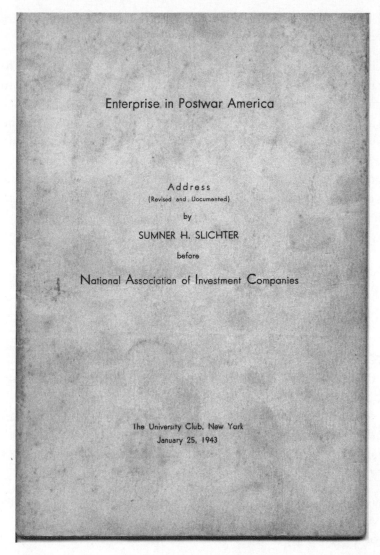

Enterprise in Postwar America

Address
(Revised and Documented)

by

SUMNER H. SLICHTER

before

National Association of Investment Companies

The University Club, New York
January 25, 1943

Professor Sumner Slichter's booklet, "Enterprise in Postwar
America"

letters in envelopes affixed with eight-cent airmail stamps and dropped
them in the campus mailbox. An enthusiastic Henry arranged to meet
Dick in New York one weekend to thrash out his ideas. Dick eagerly
registered his support. Then Henry sketched out the plan in more

detail for Leon Jr. In a six-page letter on Army Air Forces stationery in October 1944, he wrote:

> The idea in a nutshell: People all over the country will want to start businesses [after the war] and in doing so will need a certain amount of capital. At the same time others will have capital they want to invest. Dick's and my idea is to combine these needs. The person who wants to start a business, for example, will come and see us, at which time we will tell him that if he will incorporate we will get him the money. We do everything for him: the incorporating, the issuing of stock, and the sale of the stock to the people who wish to find a good investment.

The letter concluded with the following:

> I neglected to mention that our plan involves not spending any of our money, except renting an office.

Leon Jr. was not as easily convinced. He questioned how an inexperienced threesome could compete with well-established banks and brokerage firms. He also asked how three raw entrepreneurs could unearth investors willing to fork over capital to them for the purpose of funding start-ups.

Leon's practical concerns notwithstanding, Henry's beginning ideas ignited the planning process and directed the threesome's entrepreneurial spotlight on financial services. Here are more excerpts from Henry's correspondence:

> We may not have anything but an unborn idea. We haven't even begun to build around it, but as far as I'm concerned, I've got a goal to work for. My morale has been raised a thousand per cent.
>
> Of course, the start is going to be awfully rough, but really isn't that what you want—it will make everything so much more interesting and exciting. Have I convinced you?
>
> [I]n spite of our being three nobodies I think that we will succeed . . .
>
> We must all sacrifice a certain amount of pleasure to devote time to laying the foundation for our business.

What we are looking for are some stepping stones that we can build around . . .

[I]f we fail our knowledge can undoubtedly be used in some other form of business. . . .

I know that the idea and essence of this is something big, awfully big!

Passages of Dick's letters from college echo Henry's enthusiasm:

[T]he three of us must always stick together—no matter what be the course or what may come up. . . .

I see unlimited advantages in the fact that the three of us combine. We are each talented in different fields and a combination would definitely lead to success. In unity there is strength and there could be [no] more strength than in the unison of three brothers.

Right now I plan to do quite a bit more studying outside of the school than I have in the past. However, next semester I will take 21 hours which will make it a little tough, but I plan to put in plenty of time in the business. My plans are also definitely for a decrease in social pleasures in favor of studying.

Having completed half of his law school courses before entering the service, Leon Jr. articulated some of his thoughts in legalese:

[W]e should consider ourselves at the present as a "pre-business" partnership. If I get the time, I might draw up a charter and by-laws . . .

Our assets at the moment (according to our invisible balance sheet) consist of intangibles only. Among these we may list: our Strong Desires and Hopes (which has a high value at present); the sum total of our native and acquired knowledge incident to our future business (the worth of which is presently a matter of some doubt); an untold mass of ideas and opinions; and the Good Will of our parents and family. With other assets that are not so easily expressed, certainly at the moment such outweigh any of the liabilities—which means that our Proprietorship element is rich indeed.

My one great and present dream is to see the three of us together in a successful venture. Maybe we won't hit the ceiling of Heaven, but it doesn't hurt a bit to hold our ambitions high.

You and Hank are the greatest partners I could ever ask for, both in business and Life, for I know the strength of the bonds that bind us together. With the inspiration that we have received from Mother and Dad, such a course is almost a heritage[:] something we were fated to pursue from the very first.

A Tradition of Trailblazers

Henry came from a long line of self-directed, independent thinkers. His paternal grandfather, Adolph Bloch, was a genuine trailblazer. He served as a guide for the famous frontiersman, Kit Carson, on his journey to the American West. He left Carson to settle in Minneapolis, Kansas, a small prairie town that today has 2,000 inhabitants. To Adolph, Minneapolis in the late 1800s felt like a good place to make a life and a living. He married, raised a family, and opened a general store.

The guide-turned-entrepreneur was also a clever marketer. An 1885 ad in the *Minneapolis Messenger* reads, "I commenced May 1st, to offer my entire stock of men's, boys', youths' and children's clothing at cost. To the doubtful, I will say that this is no humbug or scheme to increase my sales . . . A. Bloch, Destroyer of High Prices."[3] Another ad says: "Mr. Bloch does not propose to be eclipsed by anyone in the trade."[4]

Henry's father Leon was the second of Adolph's three sons. Not interested in the family's small retail business, he attended and graduated from the Kansas City School of Law (which is now part of the University of Missouri-Kansas City) at the turn of the century. One day, while working as a law clerk for 50 cents a day before graduating from law school, Leon received an unusual phone call.

"I think you're getting some of my mail," said the caller, who identified himself as an attorney and, surprisingly, also as Leon Bloch. "I would be grateful if you would change your name." The younger Leon Bloch, who had no middle name, found middle ground by giving himself one. He chose "Edwin," the last name of his boss. Mr. Edwin was no doubt impressed by his intern's permanent show of admiration.

But one day came when Mr. Edwin wasn't so impressed with his mentee. Leon had forgotten to perform one of his daily duties— making the regular bank run. After summoning the young law clerk to his office the next morning, Edwin roared, "Don't let that ever happen again!" In a calmer voice, he added, "I have decided to give you a nickel a week raise." Leon expected the scolding, but he didn't see the pay hike coming. This unforgettable conversation taught Leon that it's possible to be critical and compassionate at the same time. It also taught him to never forget another bank run.

Following law school and four years at a prominent Kansas City law firm, Leon quit to go into practice for himself. "Dad had offers to go with big law firms," Henry says, "but he always turned them down. He wanted to do what he wanted to do." Besides practicing law, Leon wanted to see the world. And he figured the only way to have that freedom was to be on his own. "For Dad, having independence was a higher priority than making lots of money."

As a sole practitioner, Leon specialized in serving low-income African Americans, a demographic segment that was generally overlooked by larger law firms. He helped his clients buy homes, he drafted wills, and he handled their legal problems. With a strong reputation in the black community for performing quality service at a fair price, Leon's practice benefited from word-of-mouth recommendations. He earned enough money to buy a few rental houses and small apartment buildings in the same neighborhoods he served. His tenants were mainly his law clients.

Henry's mother, Hortense Bienenstok, was the daughter of a St. Louis furrier. Unlike some women in the early 1900s who were subservient to their husbands, Horty was fiercely independent and strong-minded, yet an exceedingly loving wife and mother. Thirteen years younger than Leon, who was 39 when they married, she had a thirst for philosophy that remained unquenched.

As Dick wrote in his unpublished memoirs, "She read and reread [Emerson's] works like some people would read the Bible. She believed that doing the right thing every day of your life was much more important than asking for forgiveness."

Her uncle Henry Wollman, a senior partner in the firm at which Leon had worked, introduced them to each other. Horty was no doubt happy to trade in her awkward last name when she married Leon, even though her new surname would be forever misspelled and mispronounced. (Erroneously, "Bloch" is often written phonetically with a "k" instead of an "h," and it is commonly enunciated as "Blotch.")

"My folks took their honeymoon in Virginia Beach," Henry says. "Dad loved trains. He figured out the longest way to get there from Kansas City. It was the same fare as the most direct route."

Horty's side of the family had its share of pioneers. A portrait of her maternal grandmother, Betty Wollman, hangs in the Kansas State Historical Society in Topeka. A plaque with three short lines affixed to the frame explains her celebrated life:

> One of Kansas' Earliest Settlers
> Abraham Lincoln Visited Her
> Home at Leavenworth in 1859

Betty once described the role of women during the days of the Old West: "The hardships were many, and the courage and self-denial of the women who worked side by side with their husbands and sons and brothers in those primitive days are largely responsible for the development of the Middle Western States, now so rich in everything that goes to make life worth living."[5]

When Betty and her husband Jonas settled in Fort Leavenworth, it was purportedly the largest city between St. Louis and San Francisco. He opened and operated the town's general store. Passing through Leavenworth before becoming President, Abraham Lincoln visited the Wollman home and cradled Betty's son, Henry Wollman, in his arms.

Horty's mother, Etta, was one of nine Wollman children. Four of Etta's siblings moved to New York City, where they made their mark. Morton joined the flourishing investment bank that his brother William founded. Henry ran a prominent law practice. And Kate lived in the shadows of her three brothers' success. The four, who never married, lived together in a 22-room apartment overlooking Central Park. Kate came into a large sum of money after her three brothers died. She gave most of her inheritance to charity, including one million dollars to New York's Bellevue Hospital, the oldest public hospital in the United States. She also donated $600,000 to construct a skating rink in New York's Central Park. The Wollman Rink continues to be a popular draw, as thousands of skaters use it daily during its season.

Carrying on the Entrepreneurial Spirit

Through their written correspondence, Henry, Dick, and Leon began to map out a strategy to carry on the entrepreneurial spirit of the Blochs and Wollmans. In one of his letters in late 1944, Dick wrote:

> I believe that all details should be kept a strict secret except from our immediate family, or dad. I can see how it might be detrimental to talk to others about the details of our business, but I can't see how it could bring anything but good to ask dad any questions which might come up and to get his aid and assistance. . . .

After apprising their father of the steps they were taking to start a business, Leon Sr. encouraged his boys to blaze a trail. He wrote:

> About the future business, you may rest easy now in the thought that whatever you three boys may undertake jointly will be a great success. . . . Any plans will be worthwhile and subject to change, as the opportunities present themselves. . . . Of course, with the present conditions, you cannot plan as to time, but all will come about in due time. . . . These present days . . . will be of much greater value than you now believe. . . .

With their father's strong support, the boys were even more fervent about launching a business. But Henry cautioned his brothers that enthusiasm and creativity alone do not guarantee success in business:

> I have lots of ideas, but I'm greatly lacking in technical knowledge—which might in some way account for the ideas. . . . We all know that we greatly lack practical experience. . . . Before we open our doors *everything* must be figured out.

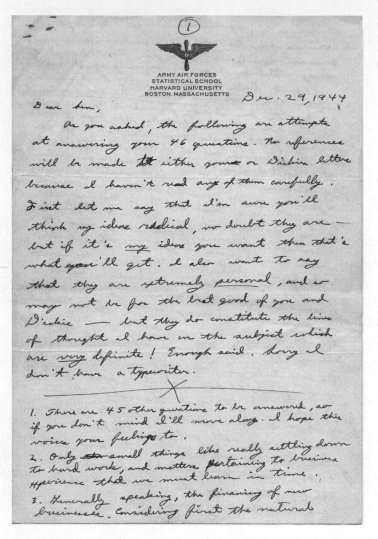

The first page of one of Henry's many long letters to his brothers about starting a business

To address their lack of business experience, Dick offered a plan:

The executive abilities possessed by myself are probably as limited as my salesmanship abilities at present, but I intend to expand them as I believe it will be necessary for each of the three of us to assume an executive position when the business grows to its ultimate size . . . after I get my degree or even before (if I don't go in the army before this summer), to get a job with an investment company and study their organization, methods, and functions. If this doesn't give me the general knowledge I desire, I plan to change companies, maybe pick a concern in New York or maybe another one in Kansas City. Right now I know a little of practical business, but before we are ready to start, I plan to know quite a bit more.

Henry's discovery of Professor Slichter's booklet represented the highlight of his Harvard education. It led to a career path, not only for him but also for his brothers. But he was committed to several more months of military service after receiving his certificate in statistical control. After all, he needed to apply his newly acquired analytical skills to organize the movement of airmen, bombers, and supplies.

Walker Army Airfield, located on the outskirts of Hays, Kansas, was the next and final stop on his military journey. Crews for the new B-29 bomber were trained during the war at its expansive facility there with three runways, auxiliary gunnery ranges, and bomber ranges. Henry was one of several personnel officers at the base of nearly 6,000 servicemen. Although the job didn't compare to the riveting and treacherous combat missions he flew over Germany, he still found it quite interesting.

"Out here things are better than ever," he wrote his father. "My job, which is one of the two most important ones on the field, is perfectly to my taste. . . . I do about 18 hours of work during 8 hours. To give you some idea of the importance of it, the schedules we make up determine the output of Bomb Groups—bad scheduling means little flying, good scheduling means lots of flying."

Among his most vivid memories of his stint at Walker was the day Roosevelt died. Though it was widely recognized that the war and the office were taking a toll on the president's health, it was hard for Henry to imagine a world without Roosevelt.

Following the president's demise in April 1945, Mussolini was captured in Italy, Hitler committed suicide in Berlin, German forces surrendered in Europe, and Henry was finally discharged from the Army Air Corps. Meanwhile, Dick graduated from the University of Pennsylvania, and Leon Jr. was reassigned from the Air Transport Command in Hawaii to Guam.

On July 22, 1945, Henry packed his bags and boarded a bus in downtown Hays, Kansas, the once wild and lawless town where Wild Bill Hickok was sheriff. As the bus traveled 250 miles of flat Kansas landscape, Henry looked forward to becoming a civilian. He was also energized by his dream of starting a business. That evening, two of the three Bloch brothers were united in Kansas City, destined to start a new life in a changing, hopeful, and peacetime America.

HENRY'S DEDUCTIONS

- Take time to dream. Then make your dream come true.
- Keep an open mind. No one has all the answers.
- To achieve success as an entrepreneur, persistence is as important as ambition and intelligence.

Chapter 4

Taking the Plunge

Before striking out on his own, Henry decided it was important to gain work experience in the investment services field. A local brokerage firm, H. O. Peet, needed a bookkeeper in the summer of 1945, and Henry landed the job. "I was making $110 a month," he recalls. Dick was on a parallel track. He worked in the municipal bond department of Stern Brothers, a broker-dealer located across the street from H. O. Peet. (Stern Brothers continues as an independent firm today. H. O. Peet became part of Kidder Peabody, then General Electric, followed by PaineWebber, and finally UBS.)

Both boys and their father—and Leon Jr., once he returned from the war—met downtown every Monday for lunch. Among their favorite restaurants was Bretton's, a popular eatery that was started by a rabbi. Max Bretton served 24 soups every day. Afterwards they walked to the Ararat Shrine Temple, where Leon Sr. was a member, to play pool. The Monday get-togethers were a tradition for the Bloch men for nearly 25 years. Although they didn't play eight-ball for money, Leon Jr. kept a running tally of their weekly results.

Not long after he joined H. O. Peet, Henry heard about an opening for a stockbroker at the firm. "I jumped at the opportunity," he says. "I wasn't learning much as a bookkeeper." After studying for and passing the securities exam, he opened his first account with his own, albeit negligible, savings. In an attempt to identify stocks that were poised to surge, he spotted KT, the ticker symbol for the Missouri-Kansas-Texas Railroad. The company had a major presence in Kansas City and was the first line to enter Texas from the north. According to Henry's 1946 tax return, he made 11 stock trades, four of which were in and out of KT. But the rookie stockbroker lost $259.62 of his hard-earned savings playing the market that year.

A few family members and friends entrusted Henry with a portion of their own savings. Among his first customers was one of his oldest and closest friends, Jack Nachman. As youngsters, the two boys played football on a vacant lot. As teenagers, they teamed up for Heart of America bridge competitions. Now, as young adults, they played golf each Sunday during the summer.

"Henry never liked to lose," Jack says. "But after commissions, he didn't make much money for me in the stock market."

When Leon Jr. returned from the service in January 1946, he found both of his brothers gainfully employed. So he decided to resume his law studies, even though he was more interested in starting a business with his two brothers. Three semesters stood between him and his degree. But after one semester, Leon made a proposition to Henry and Dick: "If you join me in testing the service business waters, I will suspend my law education."

"I beg you boys not to start a business," their father pleaded. "It's too risky. In the end, you'll probably have nothing to show for your hard work but disappointment."

"Dad made a complete about-face," Henry says. "He tried to convince me to stay at H. O. Peet."

"You have a shot at becoming the firm's first Jewish partner," Leon Sr. argued, suggesting that a less-chancy career was a more prudent course.

For Henry, being a stockbroker was nothing more than a job. "I'm not getting anywhere," he explained to his father. "All I do is phone clients and watch stocks go across the ticker tape." As difficult as it was to do, Henry defied his father. One year to the day after he started, he quit his job.

But the triumvirate was not meant to be. Twenty-year-old Dick had married his college sweetheart, Annette Modell, in the summer of 1946. He was also wedded to a new entrepreneurial brainstorm. It involved producing bed lamps that allowed users to read in bed while shielding light from their sleeping partner. He also wanted to manufacture covers for playpens that would prevent toddlers from throwing out their toys. Dick launched the Novelette Manufacturing Company.

Henry and Leon Jr. didn't allow Dick's novel idea or their father's altered outlook to thwart their plan to start their own business. Reflecting on the decision to move forward, Henry says, "If I were in Dad's shoes, I would have felt the same way. I left a respectable job, and Leon was two semesters shy of finishing law school. Besides, the odds weren't in our favor; most new businesses fail. I knew getting started would be difficult, but I was determined to become my own boss."

The Plan

After dispensing with fatherly advice, Henry and Leon Jr. finalized their business plan. Leon favored Henry and Professor Slichter's idea of supporting emerging businesses in the new postwar economy, but he had concerns about their ability to raise capital to invest in start-ups. He figured that offering a range of services to mom-and-pop businesses beyond investment banking represented a more practical path. Henry acquiesced.

The revised plan, which Leon typed out on 25 pages, consisted of 50 services that the duo would provide. Among them were business incorporation, decoration, display, temporary help, accounting, bookkeeping, legal, secretarial, collection, printing, design, and advertising. Number 30 was tax preparation, and the last one was a catch-all: "In addition to those listed above, [we] will perform any service or agency for a client-business, provided it is reasonably essential to the client-business and is compatible with [our] stated policies." Not specializing in a single field, they surmised, would increase the probability of attracting the most customers.

"What should we call our partnership?" Henry and Leon asked each other. On the short list were Consolidated Business Company, United Business Company, Brothers United, and Bloch Brothers Company. United Business Company was their first choice; it sounded like a solid, blue-chip organization. Leon checked the local phone book to see if

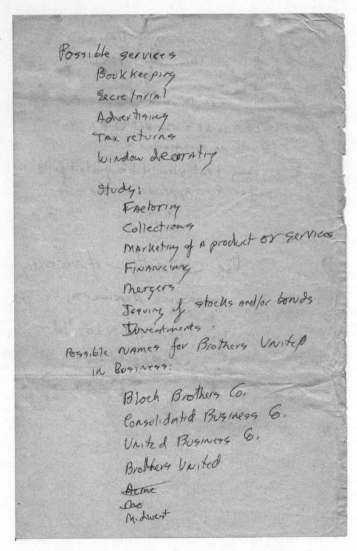

Leon jotted down possible service lines and names for the brothers' new business

the name had already been taken. Although several listings started with the word "United," there wasn't an identical match.

The organization chart for their United Business Company contemplated a staff of specialists in ten departments: finance, enterprise, investment, accounting, insurance, new business, service, small business, statistics, and research. In order to hire a team of professionals, to lease a headquarters, and to be well-capitalized, the brothers figured that they needed $50,000 in seed money. Raising that much would be impossible unless Kate Wollman, their wealthy great aunt, agreed to help. The two entrepreneur wannabes boarded a train at Kansas City's Union Station for New York City's Penn Station.

For Henry, watching the ever-changing scenery through the large train windows was as entertaining as a movie. He also enjoyed the dining car with its pressed white tablecloths and fine china. The brothers couldn't afford a stateroom, so the porter converted their seats into an upper and lower berth.

The polite doorman at the Waldorf Towers ushered them inside the elegant entry and whisked them up to the 41st floor. One of Aunt Kate's staff greeted them in the marble-tiled foyer with its elaborate crystal chandelier.

"We want to rent a big office and hire several experts," an enthusiastic Henry told his 76-year-old aunt. The plain-looking woman listened patiently to her great-nephews' grand ideas from her favorite sitting-room chair. When they finished their presentation, she mulled over their request for $50,000. After what seemed like an eternity, she countered: "I'll give you a loan for $5,000, but only if your father co-signs the note."

Negotiating any further with Aunt Kate would have been a waste of time. They walked from her apartment to the train station with the disappointing possibility of a smaller-than-desired bulge in their wallets and the aggravating caveat of their father's involvement. "So much for champagne hopes and caviar dreams," Leon Jr. glumly noted.

Quoting Emerson, their mother had once told her sons, "Finish each day and be done with it. You have done what you could." Yet it was difficult for Henry to be done with this day. At least their reluctant father went along with co-signing the note. The partners opened a bank account and deposited the $5,000 advance.

Having raised only one-tenth of the start-up funding that their plan required, the brothers had more homework to do. They composed a letter to Professor Slichter, the author of the booklet that had motivated Henry during his stint at Harvard. In August 1946, Leon Jr. wrote: "May we introduce ourselves as two young men—brothers and only recently separated from the service—who have in mind a plan involving the investment of funds and the performance of services in behalf of new business enterprises. . . . The inspiration for this plan was your address . . . a copy of which we have carefully studied and the substance of which we have thoroughly admired."

The boys were delighted when the professor's secretary called to schedule a meeting. Two weeks later, Henry and Leon Jr. packed their bags and once again took the train to Penn Station where they switched tracks for the Boston leg. Hoping the professor would advise them on a clear course of action and suggest ways to conduct a successful business, they sketched out their presentation to him during the long passage.

For Henry, walking through Harvard's centuries-old campus as a civilian in a suit and tie felt quite different from when he was a student in his military uniform. The esteemed professor politely greeted the twosome in his small, book-crammed office. Skipping the small talk, Slichter asked for a summary of their business plan. They presented their mission statement. "United shall devote itself to the business of assisting in the establishment, development and operational conduct of new enterprises, and shall provide small businesses with low-cost professional, managerial and advisory services that have been designed to eliminate business failure and to insure efficiency and security." The professor sat quietly and patiently as the brothers elucidated the 50 services they planned to market.

Leon Jr. summarizes Slichter's reaction: "After our long expedition from Kansas City for his precious advice, we got no suggestions, no encouragement. What we got was a one-liner. All the professor said was, 'Most businesses started by veterans will fail—including yours.' When Slichter said that, Henry and I couldn't wait to get out of there."

The brothers continued their quest for constructive advice. Before leaving Kansas City for Boston, they had asked a family acquaintance, who had a contact in the Truman Administration, to arrange meetings for them in Washington, D.C. (Harry Truman hailed from Independence, a part of the Kansas City metropolitan area.) After arriving in Washington and maneuvering the spacious, smoky hallways of the large limestone government buildings, they consulted with General Omar Bradley, the head of the Veterans Administration, and Henry Wallace, the Secretary of Commerce. The discussions were brief, cordial—and entirely fruitless. According to Leon, "It was another long trip home on the train. Nobody gave us any encouragement. Nobody! But we were determined."

The Start

With Aunt Kate's advance sitting in their bank account, the brothers made additional deposits. They put in their $50 monthly stipends from the GI Bill of Rights as well as their weekly bridge winnings. But with an account balance of just over $5,000, their vision of assembling a team of professionals in a prestigious office building had evaporated. Out of necessity, they scaled down their dream. They subleased a $50-a-month cubicle in the back of a real estate office on Main Street. In their cramped quarters with one table, two chairs, and a telephone, the brothers hoped to discover success.

The journey of United Business Company officially began in the fall of 1946. "On our first morning, we drove to Prospect Avenue," Henry says. "We picked it because it was a long street packed with small, unimportant businesses. Leon took one side of the street and I took the other. At the end of the day, we had nothing to show for our effort. Not a single client, not a single prospect. Zero!"

Every day, the brothers traipsed down one street after another. It was a long and dispiriting beginning. According to Henry, "These were mom-and-pop businesses. We were competing with the wives, who provided the support their husbands needed. At noon I would stop somewhere to play pinball games. Or I would go to the gym to work out. You can try selling only so long when you're getting only rejections."

Leon Jr. adds, "Every day we talked about quitting, but we never really wanted to quit. We were turned down everywhere we went, almost laughed at. They would say, 'What's your experience? What other companies do you work for? What's your expertise?' Can you imagine how discouraging that was?"

Just when Henry was thinking that his father's grim prediction might have been accurate, he caught a break. "I called on A&A, a seat-cover business on Prospect Avenue," he recalls. "Mr. Agnew, one of the owners, told me, 'I can't use you. But I have a brother who could.'" His brother ran a small hamburger stand in midtown and needed someone to keep his books. The little joint became United Business Company's first account, and its owner became the Bloch brothers' first reference.

"I think he gave us the business," Leon says, "because he felt sorry for us."

Signing up their first customer was a small milestone but hardly a steppingstone. It was such slow-going that Henry couldn't blame Leon for returning to law school at the University of Missouri-Kansas City in early 1947. But Henry, who wasn't afraid to go it alone, never considered quitting. "After all, I had no other job opportunities," he says, "and I still felt that the business could succeed." But he felt compelled to return their great aunt's $5,000 loan.

Now that he was on his own, Henry realized that it was absurd for him to promote 50 services. First, he was not qualified to provide the varied offerings. Second, he had discovered that most small businesses didn't need or couldn't afford them. So he trimmed the number to six and created a leaflet to promote his condensed menu of services: (1) bookkeeping, (2) secretarial services, (3) statement preparation, (4) collection, (5) tax preparation, and (6) insurance advising. Trudging through the streets of Kansas City, passing out flyers to small business owners, and listening to their mostly unenthusiastic feedback eventually helped Henry identify an even narrower niche—low-end, low-cost bookkeeping. It was the only service for which there was even the slightest demand. For a typical small business, he would charge a flat monthly fee of $15, which included preparation of profit and loss statements as well as payroll, sales, excise, and income-tax returns.

Henry pitched the proposal to the owner of three gas stations. "I'll think about it," the man said. He followed up a few days later, but the owner was still undecided.

Henry handed out leaflets promoting United Business Company's services

"Okay, I'll keep your books for free," an almost-desperate Henry proposed. "I hope you'll decide to pay me later, but you have no obligation." It was an offer the owner couldn't refuse. After a few months, Henry asked his nonpaying customer if he would pay him. The man consented. At $45 a month, United Business Company secured its biggest account.

Persistence and focus led to a gradual increase in accounts. It helped that Henry stood behind his work and quoted a price that no one in the market could undercut.

Henry, by the way, wasn't a trained accountant. "I enrolled in one accounting course at Michigan, but I didn't like it," he says. "So I dropped it." When he needed help with a complex accounting issue, he turned to an experienced accountant.

Still living at his parents' home, Henry was able to make ends meet. Meanwhile, Dick and Annette purchased their first house in

1947 for $11,500. It was the perfect dream home—almost. Annette didn't care for the chartreuse walls in the living and dining rooms. When Dick refused to pay to have the rooms repainted, she called his mother. Armed with a can of black paint and a brush, Horty marched over and proceeded to smear black stripes on the yellowish-green walls. Then she phoned her son at work. "Dickie, you have to come over to the house right away."

"But Mom, I'm busy," Dick replied.

"Right now!" she ordered. Dick rushed home and immediately hired a painter.

A New Partner

Horty also helped Henry solve his problems. "After gaining a few accounts, I didn't have enough time to call on prospects and also do the bookkeeping work," he says. "I put a want ad in *The Kansas City Star*. My mother was the only person to answer that ad."

"Hire your brother Dick," she instructed. Horty had always wanted her sons to go into business together. Besides, Dick's inventions hadn't taken off.

"But Dick is married," Henry said. "I can't afford to pay him what he and Annette need to live on."

"Pay him what you can," she insisted, "and I'll make up the difference."

An unconvinced Henry hired Dick. But instead of allowing his mother to subsidize Dick's salary, Henry paid Dick more than he compensated himself. "I was single and living at home, so I didn't need as much money," Henry explains.

The brothers were a productive team. Little by little, more accounts produced more revenue, allowing the brothers to make a modest living. Dick wanted to become an equal partner in the company. He took a smaller salary than Henry to pay back the advances he had previously received. After Leon Jr. finished law school, he started his own practice, which included handling the legal work pro bono for United Business Company.

The 1947 return for United Business Company showed gross receipts of $1,404.75 and net income of only $347.64

United steadily carved out a niche in the local market. Their largest competitor was a firm called Mail Me Monday. MMM was based on a different model; their clients mailed in their records weekly. The Blochs provided a more personal service by picking up and delivering their clients' documents.

Bookkeepers Henry and Dick Bloch learned how to prepare all kinds of government forms, including payroll, excise, and income-tax returns. Thanks to a detailed IRS "how-to" publication, they mastered individual income tax preparation. "Dick and I read the IRS booklet from cover to cover each year," Henry says. "Of course, taxes weren't as complicated then as they are today. Dick and I also did our own returns, and we checked each other's work."

Low customer retention rates and scanty profit margins tested the resolve of the two partners of United Business Company. In 1951, Dick stunned Henry by telling him that he had decided to quit. "Dick became an efficiency expert," Henry says, "which is a type of management consultant."

Barnett Helzberg Sr., owner of a Kansas-City based chain of jewelry stores called Helzberg Diamonds Shops, had offered Dick $100 a day as an efficiency expert. This was far more than he was making as a bookkeeper. Considering that Dick's dream had been to make $300 a month, he jumped at the opportunity. And he was quite successful. In short order, he was spending half his time on the road, consulting mainly for regional jewelry chains.

But Christmas Eve of 1952 was a defining moment for Dick's budding new career. Because his flight home from San Francisco was canceled, he missed reading "The Night before Christmas" to his children. Annette promptly informed him that his traveling days as an efficiency expert were over. Henry was delighted to welcome his old partner back.

Years earlier, after having read Professor Slichter's booklet in the Harvard library, Henry envisioned himself running a flourishing, well-capitalized business. But he realized that it was a blessing in disguise that Aunt Kate had loaned them only a tenth of what they wanted. "Our business plan wasn't realistic," he acknowledges. "If she had given us $50,000, we would have hired a big staff and leased a big office before gaining a single customer. Without a doubt, we would have gone broke within months."

Eight years after its small start, United Business Company was still in business—an accomplishment in itself. Perhaps Henry would have been further ahead if he had stuck it out at H. O. Peet. But that didn't matter. "As long as I could make a living," he says, "I wouldn't trade being my own boss for anything!"

HENRY'S DEDUCTIONS

- Determine and follow your own path. Ignore the naysayers.
- Reassess and adjust your plan as necessary.
- Never think about failing. When you fall, get back on your feet.

Chapter 5

Made in Heaven

Henry agreed to take Marion Helzberg to the engagement parties only as a favor. Normally, 27-year-old Henry's social life consisted of an occasional game of golf or bridge. Otherwise, he was married to his work. But when his dear friend, Jim Helzberg, called that spring day in 1950, Henry could not refuse. Jim was due to be married in July and Henry had already promised to be his groomsman.

"Hank, I want you to take Marion to the engagement parties for Rosine and me," Jim said. "She's coming in from college and will need a date."

Henry hardly knew Marion, a redheaded kid eight years his junior. The last time he remembered seeing her was five years earlier, when he was on leave from the Army Air Corps. When he had stopped by the Helzbergs' house in his military uniform to visit Jim, Henry made eye contact with Marion only long enough to say hello.

Henry gallantly agreed to escort her to the parties. On the evening of the first celebration, he sighed as he left work an hour earlier than usual. His desk was stacked with client records and partially completed forms. Bracing himself for a long, boring evening, he drove home, showered, and grumbled as he put on a suit and tie.

Marion, who was finishing her junior year at the University of Missouri, took a two-hour bus ride from the Columbia depot to the Kansas City station, where her mother picked her up.

"I wasn't really interested in going to all those parties," Henry admits. He got nervous on first dates, and he figured he had nothing in common with Marion. Reluctantly, he drove his green 1947 Buick convertible one mile to the Helzbergs' house to pick up Marion. Her father answered the door and cordially welcomed Henry inside.

Marion's father Morton was Henry's dentist. "He was a cheerful man who always sang or whistled as he worked on my teeth," Henry recalls. Morton was also president of the temple to which the Helzberg and Bloch families belonged.

As Henry watched Marion come down the stairs, he was struck by how beautiful she had become. Her red hair was stunning. Her eyes were gentle and kind. She greeted him with a warm smile.

"I don't remember a thing about the parties for Jim," Henry recalls, "because I was absolutely smitten with Marion. I had never known anyone like her." Used to being tense on first dates, Henry was completely comfortable. They talked, danced, and laughed.

Marion was also attracted to Henry. "I've had an eye for you ever since I saw you at our house in your military uniform," she later told him.

Henry wasn't the only one who was enthralled by Marion's charm and attractiveness. Cousin Charles Helzberg says, "There is something special about Marion. She's an absolute knockout. And she's very warm and caring—a beautiful woman. I never remember one negative word coming out of her mouth."

Henry's old friend, Dick Levin, feels the same way. "She's very attractive, but never a siren. Marion is much more the girl next door. Besides being so darn good-looking, she happens to have a wonderful manner about her. It's crazy—she is such a beautiful *and* nice person! And underneath that beauty is a very tenacious woman."

The Courtship

All of a sudden Henry had an interest more important than his United Business Company. Every weekend he drove to Columbia, or Marion rode the bus to Kansas City. On occasion Dick Levin and his girl-friend, Carol Hoffman, accompanied Henry to Columbia.

One weekend the two couples attended a formal dance at Marion's sorority house. Just before the threesome departed for the return trip to Kansas City, Carol planned a practical joke. "We kidnapped Marion," Dick says. "Initially, we were going to take her a block or two. Then Carol and I egged on Henry to take her back with us to Kansas City. It was a lark."

Marion was not amused. "She was supposed to be in school," Dick explains. After her continual demands to be returned to campus fell on deaf ears, Marion pulled out a nail file from her purse and proceeded to cut a hole in the cloth top of the convertible. Henry suddenly felt terrible, not so much about the tear but about how upset he had made Marion. After demanding that she be dropped off at the bus station in the next town, Henry finally submitted to her wishes. Taking stock of the incident, Dick says, "It was so wrong of us. It was irrational." Nonetheless, the couples reminisced about the episode for years. Henry would never again partake in a practical joke on his sweetheart.

Marion and Henry

Following a five-month, long-distance courtship, the couple talked seriously about marriage. "I'll never forget going to her parents' home and asking her father for permission to marry his only daughter," Henry says. "Even though he had been my dentist since I was a kid, I was plenty nervous. But he made it easy. He told me that from now on my dental work would be free. And he also told me that he wanted me to prepare his tax returns. Incidentally, I found a few mistakes on his prior returns that were prepared by a CPA."

Henry could hardly afford to get married. He had practically no savings, and he was making just enough to get by. It was a classic case of true love clouding rational judgment. The couple was engaged on January 27, 1951. Though he didn't get on one knee or surprise her, Henry did present Marion with an eye-catching diamond ring that he had bought through a friend in the jewelry business.

During the months before their wedding, the two lovebirds fired off passionate letters to each other in between frequent and lengthy long-distance phone calls and weekend rendezvous. The following excerpts come from different letters that Henry wrote Marion.

> Beautiful, if you only knew how much I love you. I look at your picture all the time I'm in the office—and consequently I don't get much work done.
>
> Baby, why do you make me miss you so much? It makes it awfully difficult to concentrate on my work, or for that matter anything else. Believe me, you've got me wound around your little finger (like a yo-yo).
>
> [My dog] Scrappy is lying on my bed staring at me and panting—just like I do when I think of you.
>
> This morning I told a few clients and the people at the office that I was engaged—and they nearly died. They all kept reminding me of how I was such a confirmed bachelor. I never thought that I would ever be so completely in love with any- one (except Scrappy). Did I ever tell you that you have quite a way with men—especially this *one*.
>
> I'm so glad we announced our engagement instead of waiting. I know that we couldn't have possibly kept it a secret. It's difficult enough now when we're out in public and I can't squeeze you in my arms.

Just one month from now we will be Mr. & Mrs.—and right now I suppose we will be with a line a mile long of people congratulating us. And then, a few hours later our honeymoon begins—and I will be privileged to spend the rest of my life loving you. And, *believe me*, that won't be hard to take.

My dearest love, I do believe that no man has ever felt such love and honor towards his fiancée. May our next hundred years together help me to prove it. You are beautiful, intelligent, sweet, and with a wonderful personality. And much, much more than I could ever deserve.

I really believe we need another man in the office, because after we're married I'd rather not work so hard. In fact I would prefer to retire and play with you at night and in the morning and golf in the afternoon. It's going to be difficult to find time to do work.

Marion demonstrated a similar passion for Henry. Again, these excerpts are taken from different letters:

[My roommate] said that I talked in my sleep last night and that it was most entertaining. I went into a long dissertation about my favorite subject—'twas you. My, this talking in the sleep business must stop, or else it may prove a wee-bit embarrassing. (As it was, however, I said nothing last night that couldn't be printed on the first page of the Kansas City Star.)

I'm awfully proud of you, baby. You have done so great in your business, which proves you can do anything you set out to do. However, darling, I never want you to work too hard, because there's nothing more important to me than your health.

As I sit here rhapsodizing to you, the radio is playing a most timely and appropriate song—"Homesick for You." And honey, that's *just* what I am. Honest to goodness sweetheart, I miss you so much. Really, to be separated from you is as bad as onions separated from hamburgers. Seriously though, I'm in a mighty bad state.

The Union

On June 16, 1951, one month after Marion's college graduation, the 28- and 20-year-olds married in a lovely, formal, outdoor ceremony at Oakwood Country Club in Kansas City, Missouri. The Helzbergs and Blochs were members of the club, which had been founded decades earlier by a group of Jewish families. Henry had joined following the war when it offered a reduced initiation fee of $50 for veterans.

After Henry slipped the wedding band on Marion's ring finger, she vowed to herself to never remove it for as long as she lived. Their

Marion and Henry were married on June 16, 1951

friends thought this was a marriage made in heaven. "There's no question about it," friend Jean Nachman says. "It is one of a kind. Nothing is missing. It's so beautiful."

The newlyweds flew away the next morning on their honeymoon, and Henry's father helped pay for the trip. Their flight reservations were neither first class nor coach; the couple went on a cargo plane. Sitting on hard boxes for three hours was at least easy on the pocketbook. Upon their arrival in New York, they were treated to a swell dinner on Aunt Kate Wollman's fine china in her grand apartment. The next morning the newlyweds boarded a steamship for the two-day trip to Bermuda. Their accommodations weren't luxurious, but at least the second leg of their trip wasn't on a cargo ship.

Marion wrote a letter to both sets of parents from the Elbow Beach Surf Club. "We arrived at this little bit of paradise early last evening. We got cleaned up, had dinner, and danced on an opened-roof terrace. . . . Married life is out of this world. My husband is the greatest—the most precious and adorable man on earth. Mom and Dad, the wedding was truly wonderful and we are really thankful to you for giving us such a gorgeous wedding."

In contrast with Aunt Kate's spacious residence in a distinguished high-rise, Henry and Marion moved into a modest, one-bedroom unit at Twin Oaks, a pair of 11-story redbrick apartment buildings in midtown Kansas City. Because they were the first occupants of their unit, the walls had yet to be painted. "We invited our friends to a painting party," Henry recalls. "They began to play tic-tac-toe all over the walls, and Marion got concerned that their markings would show through. We finally got the place painted and it looked fine."

The Family

Three months into their marriage, Marion got pregnant with their first child. When it became obvious they would quickly outgrow the apartment, Henry wanted to design their first house. "It was the worst thing you ever saw," he now admits. "The drawing looked like a shoebox, with bedrooms in the basement." Fortunately, his father talked him out of it.

An architect came up with a traditional 1950s style, split-level brick house with three bedrooms—none of which were in the basement. Henry took out a three percent mortgage and had the house built on a lot just across the state line in Kansas for $25,000. "I ran out of money when we were finishing the driveway," Henry says. "Dad loaned me $1,000 and I signed a note for it. However, he never asked me to repay him." But Henry repaid his bank loan as soon as he could. "I hated having debt." The Blochs moved in to their new house on the very day that Marion and their newborn son were released from the hospital. Marion's mother had unpacked their boxes and helped the new family settle in.

Henry developed an unusually close relationship with his in-laws. "Marion had a simple upbringing," he says. "Her parents didn't have much money, even though her father worked very hard. Morton stopped by our house on his way home from work every night. He loved holding his only grandchild. And like clockwork, on the 16th of every month, our wedding anniversary date, we received a postcard from him. The Helzbergs were a very affectionate family."

In one postcard, Morton wrote: "Sunday is your wedding anniversary! Both of you must realize what I think of you and what you mean to me. . . . Your union is on the firmest of foundations and I am confident that your future will be blessed with great happiness and contentment. Believe me, I am very proud of the Henry W. Bloch family."

Horty Helzberg was a loving mother and a fabulous cook. She frequently had Marion and Henry over for dinner, after which Morton played his mandolin. "Marion and her mother were inseparable," Henry says. "They talked on the phone every single day, usually more than once."

Out of necessity, the young Bloch family was thrifty. When Henry finally splurged on a second car, he bought Marion a used Studebaker for $50. And when Marion's brother, Howard, got married in Birmingham, Henry could afford only one round-trip plane ticket. Marion attended the wedding while Henry stayed home and worked. Still, the newlyweds had a good life.

"Marion used to put too much food on the table," Henry complains. "I weighed 145 pounds on our wedding day. One year later I weighed 170."

The groom made only one request of his bride: Learn how to play bridge and golf. Though she attempted both, Marion didn't care a bit for either. But she kept herself plenty busy. Over a seven-year period during the 1950s, she gave birth to four healthy children—Robert, Thomas, Mary Jo, and Elizabeth. Although she may have let her husband down by not mastering his two favorite games, she was one stupendous mother.

While Henry ran his office, Marion ran her household. "She wasn't at all interested in hearing about what was going on at the company," Henry says. "The business didn't mean a thing to her." Marion made sure that both of their personal lives revolved around the family.

The Blochs were part of a close group of young Jewish couples. In postwar Kansas City, Jews were often excluded from the broader social scene. Country clubs, for instance, had restricted memberships. So Jews formed their own establishments.

"On Friday nights, we went out for a movie and dinner, usually with another couple," Henry explains. Among their favorite films were *Singin' in the Rain* with Gene Kelley, Bing Crosby's *White Christmas*, and *Guys and Dolls* starring Frank Sinatra. One of their top restaurants to go to after a movie was Fred Harvey's. Operating a café in Kansas City's Union Station and other train terminals across the country, Fred Harvey is thought to have founded the nation's first "chain" restaurant. Mr. Harvey had a policy of hiring waitresses, not waiters. The Harvey Girls, as they were known, had to be single and from 18 to 30 years old. The charcoal-broiled lamb chops with whipped potatoes and a salad cost around $2, and a slice of apple pie was about 25 cents. The couple also enjoyed the coffee shop at the Muehlbach Hotel. It was the biggest hotel between Chicago and the West Coast. Every president from Woodrow Wilson to Richard Nixon stayed in its Presidential Suite.

Once a month, Henry and Marion met with their poker group. The Saturday night game rotated from house to house. The men played at the dining-room table and the women put a couple of card tables together. "Marion loved being with the girls, but she was not much of a card player," Jean Nachman says. "She could never remember how the hands are ranked. Henry had to write it out for her—one pair, two pair, three of a kind, all the way up to royal flush. Antes were 25 cents, and bets were 50 cents. If you won four or five dollars in a night, you were doing well." The game always ended at midnight, when the hosts served dinner.

Jean recalls one of the midnight dinners at the Blochs' home. "Henry was trying to carve a ham but was butchering it. I said to Jack, who carves like a doctor, 'You've got to take over.'" Henry was happy to be relieved by a pro. For dessert, Marion made an upside-down pineapple cake, but she mistakenly made it right-side up.

In addition to raising four children, Marion became involved in her community. Committed to the education of each of her kids, she was president of the PTA at Prairie Elementary School. She served on the Women's Committee of the New Reform Temple and the Temple board. And, as an admirer of fine dance, she served on the board of the State Ballet of Missouri.

Dick Levin says, "Marion and Henry are a perfectly suited couple, and their devotion to each other is obvious."

Henry gives her all the credit. "She is a great woman—a wonderful wife and magnificent mother. Marion has always made me so happy. She is perfect."

HENRY'S DEDUCTIONS

- Love is a gift. Treasure it.
- In everything you do, give it your all.
- If you give your best, the best comes back to you.

Chapter 6

A Blockbuster Idea

"In every successful business, luck plays a part in the story," Henry Bloch says. But during the first eight years of his entrepreneurial experiment, he had little success and even less luck.

It was a long, hard slog. Henry's first partner, his older brother Leon Jr., left a few months after their start-up tried to take off. For Leon, finishing law school seemed a more sensible plan than investing more time in their fledgling concern. There was hardly a day in 1947 that 24-year-old Henry didn't wonder whether carrying on was futile. But he stuck it out. "I had nowhere else to go and nothing else to do," he says.

His next partner, his younger brother Dick, also quit. But after a stint as a management consultant, Dick came back. Together, the two bookkeepers fought to make their business profitable. They persevered, but the enterprise didn't exactly prosper.

There were some hard-won accomplishments. By the mid-1950s, the brothers were running the largest bookkeeping firm in Kansas City. With a dozen employees, mostly clerks, they were meeting a need for the smallest of small business. But they were charging rock-bottom fees for a quality service, forcing them to constantly discover ways to improve their operating efficiency. To borrow from their mother's trove of Ralph Waldo Emerson axioms, "That which we persist in doing becomes easier, not that the task itself has become easier, but that our ability to perform it has improved."

According to his income tax return, Henry made $6,000 in 1951, the fifth year of United Business Company. The following year he earned $250 more. To put these earnings in perspective, at the time a gallon of gas cost 20 cents, a flannel shirt at Sears had a price tag of $1.79, and the average annual wage based on a 40-hour workweek was about $3,000. Henry was all but doing the work of two people, trying to provide a higher standard of living for his growing family. But the outlook for his business was not promising.

"It was a terrible business," Henry explains. "We would get one new client and then we would lose one. Some of our accounts struggled to keep their doors open from one month to the next. And they couldn't always pay what they owed us." There was no enjoyment in constantly tussling with clients, attempting to extract the flat $15 monthly fee. Some would barter with them.

"Take a chair," one client offered in lieu of the monthly fee.

Constantly searching for ways to make productivity enhancements, Henry and Dick reworked their sales strategy. No more trudging up one side of the street and down the other, knocking on the doors of the most undersized commercial establishments in town. "We found out that the Chamber of Commerce regularly updated its membership roster," Henry says. "Most of the new members were start-ups. First, we would phone them for an appointment. If they agreed to meet with us, I would go to their office to make a pitch. It saved time and lots of rejections." Soon they supplemented the cold-calling program with small ads in the local newspaper.

A 60-hour or longer workweek didn't offer much of a life for a young man with a young family. In the early days of United Business Company, Henry had played bridge to make ends meet. Now he hardly had time to play anything, especially during the first quarter of each year. Miss Porter was partially responsible for his expanded work schedule.

This Tax Thing

In the late 1940s, the affable, middle-aged Miss Porter was their landlady. (The Porter Building, then one of the largest office buildings in Kansas City's midtown, is now the national headquarters of the Veterans of Foreign Wars.) One day she asked Henry a simple question: "Will you put a sign in the lobby stating that you prepare income tax returns?" Miss Porter knew that Henry and his brother were bookkeepers and also did taxes for their bookkeeping clients. She thought the service would be a welcome convenience for workers in her building.

"Of course, we would be glad to," Henry replied.

That was the first time the Blochs marketed and charged separately for tax preparation. Tax returns had always been included in the standard $15 monthly fee for bookkeeping clients. As Henry says, "It was a good retention tool."

"Because of that small sign in the lobby, we prepared the tax returns for several secretaries in the building," Henry recalls. "Our charge was $5." That's the amount the brothers thought the service was worth. But the revenue and earnings from those tax returns didn't amount to much. The next year, more taxpayers sought out the brothers' help.

But in 1951, Henry and Dick notified Miss Porter that they would not renew their lease. They simply couldn't afford the rent. A second-floor office in a two-story building at 39th and Main Street was more economical. Their new space was situated at the top of a long, narrow, and dimly-lit flight of stairs. It featured one large room and three small private offices, each with a window.

Even without a tax sign at their new office, word continued to spread that the brothers did returns for $5. According to Dick, they prepared 160 returns for nonbookkeeping clients in 1954, netting each of them about $500. But they were dog-tired, working seven days and five nights a week. (At that time, tax season ended on March 15 instead of April 15.) While Marion was delivering the couple's second child on March 14, Henry was transforming the hospital waiting room into a makeshift office to finish up returns.

Henry describes their predicament: "I thought this tax thing was tremendous and would really help our bookkeeping business. But Dick and I were devoting so much time to it that we didn't give our bookkeeping clients the type of service they expected. They were quitting on us." Something had to give.

"We decided to quit doing taxes, except for our bookkeeping clients and a few close friends," Henry says. "It was an easy decision."

The next January rolled around. Henry was expecting a much calmer tax season. When an individual taxpayer marched into their office armed with a shoebox full of tax records, Henry was armed with a stock answer: "I'm sorry, but we don't have time to do your taxes."

"But who will prepare my return?" the discontented taxpayers almost always asked. Henry didn't have a good answer. Among their most disappointed clients was John White, a display-advertising salesman.

John handled the United Business Company account at *The Kansas City Star.* "We told him we couldn't keep doing his taxes because we

John White, the display-advertising salesman who convinced
Henry and Dick to promote their tax preparation business

were too busy with our other work," Henry says. But unlike other taxpayers who were rejected by the Blochs, John didn't leave the office wondering who would handle his taxes. Instead, he was contemplating how to convince Henry and Dick to stay in the tax business.

"I returned to the newspaper office and talked to our head copy man," John says. He wanted to try an ad—not a bookkeeping ad but one for a new category. Tax preparation. No one had ever done it before. "I was tossing around in my mind how to make the ad pull. Attention-getters are good-looking women in bathing suits, small animals, babies, and cartoons. I decided on a cartoon."

The caricature depicted a man with tired eyes and a ferocious scowl. He was sweating profusely and pulling his hair out. The caption read, "I Am Doing My Own INCOME TAX!" In addition to the ad screaming a flat price of $5 for the federal and state returns, the hours were listed—8 A.M. to 9 P.M. on weekdays and 8 A.M. to 8 P.M. on weekends.

The brothers' first ad for tax preparation

A few days later, John met with Henry and Dick. "Why don't you try to make a business out of taxes before you get out of it?" he asked. "With bookkeeping, you're focused on the business market. With taxes, you're talking about the whole population. There's a lot more potential in tax preparation."

Henry listened but remained unconvinced. After John told him that one ad would cost $100, Henry did the math. "We would need to prepare 20 tax returns just to break even!" he said. Without hesitating, John smoothly upped the ante.

"I won't let you run just one ad," John countered. "You have to run two ads because with one, you would only get half the audience. You need the evening circulation and the morning circulation." Dick was inclined to give it a try. Reluctantly, Henry decided to go along.

The ad appeared in the Sunday edition of *The Kansas City Star* on the 23rd of January in 1955. The next morning, Henry was making his usual rounds. "I made calls on each bookkeeping client to pick up their checkbook and records. Then I brought them back to our office for processing. That Monday morning I called on A & A, an automobile seat-cover store."

"Your brother phoned," the seat-cover worker told Henry. "He wants you to call him. He said it was urgent." Henry borrowed the phone and dialed JE 6400.

"Hank, get back here as quick as you can!" Dick shouted. "We've got an office full of people!"

Henry ran to his car and raced back to the office, wondering whether Dick's description was accurate. After sprinting up the long flight of stairs, he glanced around the room. Dick hadn't exaggerated. Still out of breath, Henry ushered the first person in the crammed space back to his office. He prepared one return after another until the room finally emptied out. The brothers were accustomed to working late and leaving exhausted, but this evening was different. When they said goodnight to each other, they knew they were on to something big. Henry drove home feeling beat and energized at the same time. He felt more useful than he ever had.

"Despite the long waits," Henry recalls, "our clients were truly grateful for the service they received. Most of them thanked us before we had a chance to thank them." He was anxious to tell Marion about his remarkable day.

Both of Henry's young sons were fast asleep when he pulled into the garage, but Marion was fortunately still awake. Her reaction was exactly as he had expected. She was happy—for him. It sounded like he had chanced upon his first break. She knew her husband wanted to provide a more comfortable lifestyle for his family. But she was perfectly content. The daughter of a workaholic dentist who died of a heart attack at age 60, Marion only hoped that her husband didn't have to put in long hours forever.

With minimal cash, Henry and Dick had to place their bets carefully during that tax season. Building on the simple idea given to them by Miss Porter years earlier, they drove to a lumberyard to buy two sheets of 4-foot-by-8-foot plywood, small cans of black and white paint, and two paintbrushes. "We went to our parents' house to make a sign on their driveway," Henry explains. "We covered the boards with white paint. Then, in three-foot-high black letters, we painted two words: income tax. We hung it under our second-story window on Main Street. You couldn't help but see our 16-foot sign." To supplement the homemade billboard and further promote their new concern, the brothers ran the cartoon ad in the local newspaper throughout the season. And it continued to produce.

Henry and Dick hit the jackpot. "We did $20,300 in volume in 1955," Henry recalls. It was far better than any of the preceding eight years. Though they were unprepared for the deluge of taxpayers who lined up outside their second-story office on that late January day, the two brothers managed to serve every customer over the balance of the season. It required cases of adding machine tape and reams of tax forms.

"We didn't own a copy machine," Henry says. The brothers filled out the government forms by hand. Then, using carbon paper to make a copy for the client, a secretary typed the finished product.

Mostly low- and middle-income taxpayers responded to the advertising, a group that typically wouldn't have considered using the only other professional alternative—high-priced accountants. According to Henry, "Our clients didn't make much money, but they were conscientious. They wanted to pay their fair share of taxes—nothing more." During a typical tax interview, the brothers learned practically everything about their clients' financial lives. They also learned the importance of building trust.

"I was doing a return for an elderly couple," recalls Henry. "To determine if they were entitled to an extra exemption, I asked if they were at least 65 years old. Both of them replied 'No.' After I finished the return, they thanked me and left the office. A minute later, the wife came back to my office without her husband. Leaning over my desk, she whispered, 'I'm 65, but I don't want my husband to know.' I told her 'Okay, that's all I need to know. I can get you your exemption.'"

The Birth of an Industry

To seize on their newly created market opportunity, Henry and Dick wasted no time reinventing United Business Company. At the end of the 1955 tax season, they sold the bookkeeping business for practically nothing to two veteran bookkeepers in their office. "They were pleased to take over the business," Henry says, "and we were more than pleased to give it to them." Still, it was a bittersweet transaction.

The Blochs had battled for eight years to make their bookkeeping business a success. But in the end, Henry and Dick were overworked and the company's profit was undersized. Had the brothers not stumbled on income tax preparation, Henry believes they would have kept to bookkeeping. The fatalist was anything but a quitter.

With nine and a half months to prepare for the next tax season, the brothers were faced with one key question: Where should they replicate their new service? While pondering a plan of action, they received a letter from a New York City law firm. That letter forced a second question.

"Our client, United Business Service of Massachusetts, has called our attention to your ad appearing in the April 17, 1955, issue of the *Kansas City Star*," the lawyer wrote. "We are calling your attention to this matter as we have no doubt that you began to use your name without deliberate attempt to cause confusion or take advantage of the good will built up by our client. However, we must insist that you discontinue the use of this name in order to avoid confusion and damage to United Business Service."

The brothers didn't know it then, but that correspondence represented the least threatening legal problems their groundbreaking business would face as it attempted to expand. They never considered tangling with the Massachusetts' company. "Neither of us really liked the name," Henry admits. "It was generic and didn't convey anything."

"We had learned that there was nothing impressive about a name other than the reputation that it had earned," Dick wrote in his unpublished memoirs. "[All of the top CPA firms] carried individual names like Arthur Andersen, Haskins and Sells, or Touche Ross." The top brokerage services did the same.

"What do you think about calling our new business H&R Block?" Henry asked Dick in the middle of a round of golf.

They deliberately misspelled their last name for the most mundane of reasons—to avoid spelling and pronunciation errors. "We figured people would write their checks out wrong if it was H&R Bloch," Henry explains. "And you certainly wouldn't want someone to 'blotch' your tax return."

Looking back at the founding of H&R Block, Henry and Richard's breakout year clearly wouldn't have come about without John White's advertising brainchild. But the timing of the idea was almost as extraordinary as the idea itself. Henry explains: "None of us realized that the ad would run precisely when most employees received their wage statements (Form W-2) from their employers. If John had convinced us to advertise two weeks earlier, the ad would have probably failed. Instead, it hit exactly when the segment of taxpayers with less complex returns was ready to file."

The timing was right for another important reason. Each tax season the Internal Revenue Service had offered free help in its branches for individual taxpayers. "We didn't know in 1955 that the IRS wanted to get out of preparing returns, and Kansas City was the first place they were going to try it," Henry says. "It was serendipity."

So the Blochs did prepare John's tax return that year—on the house. It was the least the brothers could do for the man who helped jumpstart the industry they pioneered. "Other than marrying my wife," John acknowledges, "it was the best idea of my life."

Summing up the birth of H&R Block, Henry says, "We knew we had a winning poker hand. And we played it for all we had."

HENRY'S DEDUCTIONS

- Find a need and fill it before anyone else.
- Success is often the product of past failures.
- Be relentless, yet adaptable.

Chapter 7

New York, New York

Henry studied the map of the United States that stretched across his battered wood desk. Dick paced the worn, hardwood floor. After a year in the tax business, the brothers wanted to expand. Topeka, Kansas, and Columbia, Missouri, both nearby towns, were logical choices.

"It makes sense to stay close to home," Henry suggested, tapping a pencil against his desk. "Plus, we would have lower upfront costs in smaller cities."

Dick began to nod. Then he stopped and said, "Hank, what do you think about New York City?"

A puzzled look overcame Henry's face. "How could we oversee those offices?" he asked himself, scratching his forehead. "And how could we break even in a city where operating and rental costs are the highest in the country?" But the more he thought about it, the more intriguing he found the idea. Before Sinatra could finish crooning *New York, New York*, Henry decided, "If we can make it there, we can make it anywhere." Confident that Marion would welcome an adventure, he made an offer: "Dick, I'll open the city, but let's take turns running it during the season."

The first step was to study the New York market. "We wrote to every newspaper there, the Chamber of Commerce, and everyone else we could think of to get every scrap of evidence on the demographics of New York," Dick recounted in his memoirs. "We studied these hour after hour. We planned every detail of the operation before ever going there."

On October 1, 1955, Henry packed his bags and drove himself to New York in Dick's dilapidated, nine-year-old Buick convertible. The windows couldn't be rolled up or down. For fresh air, the glass panels had to be removed by hand and placed on the back seat. Even worse, the jalopy didn't run in reverse. Contending with these defects, he and the car endured the 1,200-mile trip over two long days. Lacking a reservation, he chanced upon an inexpensive-looking hotel in Manhattan. After a solid night's sleep, he tackled his first assignment—to find a rental house for his family of four.

Henry scanned the classified section of the *New York Times* and saw a listing in Scarsdale, a suburb of Westchester County. Nestled between large trees on a spacious lot at the top of a hill, the attractive Tudor on a quiet street had a two-story dollhouse in the backyard. The homeowner, an attorney, was on temporary assignment in the Philippines. The place sounded perfect—except that it rented for $400 a month, about twice what he wanted to spend. Considering his father was still sore that he had quit his job at H. O. Peet, Henry didn't dare ask his parents for a loan. But Marion's mother, now a widow, offered to take out an advance against her life insurance policy to help the couple make ends meet. After the lease was signed, Marion and their two sons flew to New York.

Marion adored the house and the lovely area. Each morning she drove Henry the half mile to the train station. While he scouted out office vacancies in the five boroughs, she enjoyed pushing Robbie and Tommy in a carriage through the winding roads of the small village. She made the acquaintance of nannies and maids at a park while her boys played with neighborhood children.

The couple enjoyed Scarsdale, although they no doubt lived more modestly than their neighbors. One day the Blochs received a harsh letter from the mayor, demanding that they remove the overabundance of leaves in their yard. Although Henry hadn't budgeted for lawn maintenance, he grudgingly hired someone. Another day Marion brought home a colossal rib roast from the meat department of Gristede's, an upscale grocery store specializing in gourmet foods. Before she shoved it in the oven, Henry exclaimed, "Dear, there's no way we can afford it!" Hesitantly, she drove back to the store and handed the butcher the roast, her receipt, and a sincere apology.

As planned, the family stayed in Scarsdale for three months. Marion, eight months pregnant, then returned to Kansas City with the couple's two sons. Henry leased an inexpensive room at the Lexington Hotel in Manhattan for the tax season. He and Dick took turns staying there, commuting between Kansas City and New York every three weeks. "The room opened on an air shaft, so the only way we could find out what the weather was like would be to call the front desk," Dick recalled. "We had no way of knowing if it was raining or snowing."

When Annette visited Dick, she shopped for the least expensive laundry. Most places hung a sign in the window promoting the price of laundering shirts. "She found one within a block where shirts were 29 cents," Dick explained. But he discovered after picking up his clothes that a pair of socks was a whopping 60 cents. "That's the way people do business in the Big Apple."

The Second Season

Henry was elated when the Internal Revenue Service announced during the off-season that it would stop preparing tax returns for free at its New York City branches. That was the same lucky break that the Blochs received the year before in Kansas City. "When taxpayers get turned down at the IRS," Henry knew, "they will come directly to us." He located his seven offices, each with a four-month lease, as close as possible to the IRS branches in Brooklyn, the Bronx, Queens, Manhattan, and Long Island. The office at 144 Nassau Street served as his primary outpost. To furnish the storefronts, he purchased inexpensive card tables and folding metal chairs. And no tax office in the 1950s would be complete without bulky, crank-driven adding machines.

"We designed a lease for four months with three two-year options," Dick stated. "It was a ridiculous thing to ask for, but our philosophy was that if you don't ask, you can't receive. So we asked. We had these leases printed for a few dollars and made out like they were the standard for our business. And do you know what? Nearly everyone went along with them."

Henry wanted to hire men who exuded confidence and knew taxes. In early December, he placed a help-wanted ad in the *New York Times*.

"Do you like people and working with numbers?" he asked each of the applicants. Based on their responses, Henry selected 14 preparers. He offered them $1 an hour, which was the minimum wage, plus a potential bonus to be determined at the end of the season.

On January 2nd, the opening day of tax season, Henry rode the subway to inspect his new offices. But to his astonishment, the door was locked and the lights were off at the first office. With keys to all seven offices on his keychain, he rushed inside, turned on the lights, and phoned the preparer who was supposed to be at work. The man's wife explained that her husband had found another job. Henry dashed to the other offices only to find that some of them were also closed. "I hired employees too early!" an infuriated Henry realized. "They didn't bother to tell me they had found other jobs." After expecting a smooth season opening, Henry got the opposite. Thank goodness tax season always starts slowly. Immediately he called the *New York Times* to place a second ad.

Hiring qualified tax preparers was never easy. "Each applicant, we soon learned, claimed to know every facet of tax preparation," Dick wrote. "To ascertain the extent of their knowledge, we asked them four very simple but technical questions. . . . In one minute we could tell whether they knew taxes or they were full of hot air."

In late January, Henry returned to Kansas City for three weeks. One day while overseeing the three local offices, he took time out to drive Marion to Menorah Hospital to deliver their first daughter, Mary Jo. Not long after bringing mother and baby home, it was time for Henry to swap places with Dick. Fortunately, Marion's mother Horty was a terrific surrogate parent in Henry's absence.

"For such a big city, New York can get awfully lonely," Henry says. And it can also be a tough place to get around. "I remember taking the subway for the first time. Everyone was rushing onto the platforms. After finally figuring out which line to take, I didn't simply walk onto the train when the door opened—I was shoved onto it."

But taking the subway was preferable to driving his defective old car that couldn't go in reverse. Once Henry parallel parked near a street corner, certain that no one could pull in front of him. But his plan was foiled. When he tried to leave, he found a car parked in front of his Buick. He had no choice but to wait nearly two hours for the other car to pull out.

Without much money to spend on advertising, Henry relied on signage in the office windows identifying his company, the service, and the price. Since the office in Jamaica was a second-story location without street-level visibility, window signs were not an option. He hired a sandwich man to walk back and forth in front of the building during the early part of the season. The human billboard, which read INCOME TAX $5, proved essential.

In February and March, customers marched into the offices at an ever-increasing rate. Many of them, as expected, had been turned away by the IRS. Marion visited Henry for a couple of days at the height of the season while her mother took care of the children. But there was no time for the couple to sightsee or take in a Broadway play. Henry recruited Marion to file customer receipts in the Nassau Street office.

On the last day of the season, several tax preparers took home the expensive adding machines, even though the equipment didn't belong to them. Staring, aghast, at the empty desktops on March 16th, Henry began phoning preparers at home. "I won't return it until you pay my bonus," the tax pros promised.

"As soon as I handed out the checks," Henry says, "they gladly handed over the machines."

The seven-office New York complex generated $65,786.50 in tax preparation fees, amazingly close to the $65,000 that the brothers had projected. That total was almost $9,000 more than the three Kansas City offices produced in their second year. The hometown offices turned a profit while the New York operation, as planned, broke even.

"We knew our business," Dick declared.

All of Henry's expectations in 1956 were met—except one. He had planned to promote a tax preparer to manage New York the

H&R Block started out on the second floor at 3937 Main Street in Kansas City

following season. But there was no one with the expertise. Since neither brother wanted to uproot his family, Dick suggested selling the operation. Henry agreed.

An ad in the *New York Times* yielded a single response. Dick negotiated the sale of the rights to the nation's largest metropolitan area, including portions of New Jersey and Connecticut, to two local CPAs. The buyers wrote a check for $10,000, which was all they could afford, and agreed to pay 2 percent of future revenues. The sellers, who had hoped the business would fetch a higher price, could at least take comfort in knowing their commuting would come to an end.

"It turns out that we were among the pioneers of franchising." Henry says. "But at that time, we had never heard the term." (McDonald's first franchise opened three years earlier in Phoenix.)

After the transaction was completed, the brothers pulled into a filling station in anticipation of making another sale. Dick asked the attendant if he would be interested in buying the old Buick. After a quick inspection and a brief negotiation, the brothers pocketed $25.

Hoping the attendant wouldn't suffer buyer's remorse, the brothers ran to the subway station.

Henry purchased a used Chevy station wagon to drive back to Kansas City. With three young children, Marion needed a bigger car. Buying it in New York saved him the cost of a plane ticket home. When he pulled into his driveway two days later, his face beamed as Marion, with their two-month-old baby girl in her arms and their two sons at her side, rushed outside to greet him. Marion was pleased to have the large wagon with its ubiquitous fins and egg-crate grill, but she was even happier to have Henry back home.

HENRY'S DEDUCTIONS

- To hit a home run—in business as in baseball—timing is critical.
- If you don't ask, you can't receive.
- Luck favors those who work hard.

Chapter 8

Building Blocks

I n the spring of 1956, the two brothers charted a course for H&R Block's third year. Compared to the frenzy of the tax season, the off-season was relatively calm. "People felt sorry for us because we were in such a seasonal business," Henry says. "But it was a luxury to sit back, analyze our successes and failures, and create plans."

The 1957 plan included plowing all of the profits from the Kansas City offices into two new markets—Columbia, Missouri, and Topeka, Kansas. With the promise of a salary of $500 a month for five months and half the profits, two of their top Kansas City preparers were picked to open the towns. Since their salaries didn't begin until January, the new managers had no choice but to find part-time work elsewhere during the off-season.

Promoting standout preparers to launch new markets worked remarkably well, even though many of them had no previous management experience. But this expansion strategy by itself would take too many years and too much capital to penetrate the country.

"We opened as many offices as we could afford," Henry says. "When we ran out of money, we granted franchises." Franchising didn't require much capital from the Blochs. Except for forms, manuals, and advertising materials, franchisees supplied virtually everything, including the people and places to operate the business.

Dick was a first-rate salesman. He took on the job of signing up franchises while Henry focused on the growing and profitable Kansas City market. Instead of selling geographic areas as they had done in New York City, they gave away franchise territories. In return, the Blochs received an ongoing royalty, usually less than 5 percent of revenues. Trying to sell franchises, they decided, would sharply limit the pool of potential qualified operators.

Thumbing through the Oklahoma City phone directory in the summer of 1957, Dick randomly called owners of local accounting firms, hoping at least one would jump at the chance to join the budding tax chain. But every one of them was thoroughly disinterested. "I couldn't possibly take on more clients," the busy accountants responded. Besides, they had never heard of H&R Block.

"They failed to see what we saw," Henry says. "We were not in the business of preparing tax returns. We were in the business of the business of preparing tax returns. There's a big difference." Instead of doing the taxes, the brothers were now doing the hiring, training, leasing, marketing, and occasionally even the janitorial work. "We weren't really looking for accountants. We were looking for entrepreneurs."

Finally, Jim Thompson, an operator of three accounting offices, offered to meet with Dick in Oklahoma City. "I signed the contract because Dick was such a good salesman," Jim says. "He told me it would prove to be the smartest move I ever made. At first, I wasn't so sure. But he was right."

Dick followed a similar strategy in Little Rock, Arkansas, and Des Moines, Iowa. In subsequent years, he and Henry relied mostly on newspaper ads to recruit franchisees. The advertisements invited prospects to a meeting at a local hotel to learn about H&R Block. It was a more efficient way to unearth good operators. As the Block name became recognizable and the brothers could show their recruits the track record of established tax offices, more people showed up at the get-togethers.

Entrepreneurship 101

Henry and Dick tried to impart a simple philosophy to each franchisee. First, do the finest work possible. Second, charge fairly. And third, give the customers more than they expect. Serving the most clients, rather than making the most money, was of the utmost importance.

"Instead of figuring out how much we wanted to *earn* from each tax return, we figured what the service was *worth* to the consumer," Henry says. "Then we figured out how to stay in business by charging that amount."

The vast majority of returns prepared in Block offices cost $5, although an unusually complex filing may have warranted as much as $10. Besides creating a compelling value proposition and high customer loyalty, low prices established a barrier to entry. "We were worried about competitors coming into our market," Henry says. "That's why we never talked publicly about how well we were doing. People always asked, 'How can you afford to stay in business by charging only $5?'"

"The early franchisees took a leap of faith," Henry says. "They were businesspeople who were willing to take a risk. As they helped us expand the brand geographically, they were also helping us create a winning formula. Some of the best ideas came out of our operations meetings with them."

One suggestion was to give clients a "TaxSaver," a large envelope in which they could store and categorize their tax records throughout the year. Another idea related to pre-addressed mailing envelopes for the clients' federal and state returns. Complications arose when clients mistakenly placed the federal return in the state envelope, and vice versa. "Print the federal envelope in black ink and the state envelope in green ink," someone advocated. "Color-coding proved to reduce careless errors."

Unlike at traditional CPA firms, H&R Block preparers completed the taxes in front of their clients. The brothers knew that their clientele was anxious to know the tax balance due or refund amount before leaving the office. One week later, taxpayers could pick up their finished returns or receive them in the mail. In the interim, a messenger hauled the returns to a central processing center where a tax theory checker and a math checker each reviewed the forms for accuracy.

Then a machine operator made copies of the forms for the clients and the taxing agencies. The assembled returns were couriered back to the retail outlets.

During the summer, the brothers began writing a policy and procedure manual for distribution to each city manager and franchisee. As new rules and practices were adopted, they mailed out revised pages of the P&P to the field offices. Eventually, the "how-to" manual consisted of several thick three-ring binders that took up an entire bookshelf. One of the bigger volumes was devoted to locating and setting up tax offices. Another focused on employee training. The goal was to create an effective, standardized, and efficient operational network.

According to the P&P, one tax desk, which was originally 36 inches by 60 inches, could generate $5,000 in tax fees during the season. But to improve operating efficiencies, new desk models were specially made to accommodate multiple preparers. A five-person desk, for instance, was 30 inches by 20 feet, with four glass panels two feet high dividing the stations. Practically all supply items—staplers, ashtrays, pencils, men's neckties, radios, wastebaskets, tax forms, and so forth—were printed with the H&R Block logo on them.

"Whether you go to a Block office in Oklahoma City or Kansas City, your experience should be the same," Henry says. "The P&P was our Bible."

In those days, males dominated medicine, law, and even accounting. But one day, a woman from a rural town in northern Missouri walked into Henry's office, seeking a position as a tax preparer. "I filed all my farmers' returns," the woman told Henry. "I'd like a job with you."

Henry asked her several questions to determine if she knew taxes. "After answering each one as if she had written the tax code," Henry recalls, "I couldn't turn her down." She proved to be a superstar.

Henry didn't hesitate to hire additional women, even though some male chauvinists in the organization questioned the practice. But they quickly came around once they saw how dependable, conscientious, and service-oriented the women were. In a few years, the majority of tax professionals would be women.

With a growing demand for skilled preparers, training became an increasingly critical facet of the operation. To develop a pool of tax pros, Henry taught continuing education classes at Rockhurst University and at the University of Missouri-Kansas City. But the ultimate solution was to operate a school in the branch tax offices before each season.

Henry didn't shy away from new ideas to improve the operation. Someone said, "If you always do what you've always done, you'll always get what you've always gotten." But sometimes, new ideas were not the answer.

While amending his father-in-law's returns, Henry discovered that the CPA made the identical mistake every year. To avoid such problems, Henry resolved that individual preparers should never serve the same clients in consecutive years. The next January he ordered his veteran Kansas City preparers to switch offices so they would work with a completely different set of clients.

"It was a terrible idea," Henry confesses. When clients walked in and asked for their previous preparer, they were told he or she no longer worked at that location. "It's like going to a doctor; we might be better off seeing someone different, but we become loyal to the professional who earns our trust."

Henry learned his lesson. "It's not what you or I think that's important; it's what the customer thinks," he told his associates. "The customer is the most important person in the organization."

During the height of the season, Henry worried that clients were waiting in the jam-packed offices more than an hour to be served.

"Dick, let's stop advertising until we catch up," he suggested.

"Never!" Dick countered. "We will *never* stop advertising."

"Dick was absolutely right," Henry now says. "We had to address our operating problems without sacrificing growth."

To contend with long waits, customers were offered complimentary coffee. Soothing music played on a radio, and lollipops were given to children. The brothers also instituted a number system. As soon as preparers became available, they would call out the next number.

"But using numbers was very impersonal," Henry decided. "We went to a list so that we could call clients by name." Then someone suggested offering appointments so customers wouldn't have to wait. Everybody in the organization thought it was a great idea. But when clients who had appointments walked in and got served before clients without an appointment, those who had been waiting got up and left. The brothers learned the value of testing ideas before adopting them system-wide.

With their name on the door of every office, Henry and Richard (H and R) were fanatical about providing quality service. As they told new preparers, "We want each client to say, 'Thank you. That's a fine job you did for me.' If they don't, then we've failed."

To minimize the chance of failure, the brothers gained as much knowledge as they could about their customers and their needs. For example, they discovered that taxpayers have fairly predictable filing patterns. January filers, who represented only 5 percent of the total, were mainly the elderly and self-employed. Procrastinators included higher-income earners, young people, and individuals whose tax records were less organized. The Blochs created a painstakingly precise scheduling system for each office by morning, afternoon, and evening segments based on daily, weekly, and monthly historical client flow patterns.

By understanding and anticipating their customers' needs, the duo built a strong foundation. With 17 offices in three states in 1957, the company began using the slogan, "Nation's Largest Income Tax Service."

When asked about the secret of their success, Henry replied, "We give people peace of mind."

Leon Sr., who a decade earlier had pleaded with his sons not to start their own business, now hung an oversized map of the United States on his office wall. Whenever an H&R Block office opened in a new city, he stuck a pin in the map, as though he were a general marking a victory after a hard-fought battle.

"Dad was awfully proud of us," Henry says. "I can't blame him for having tried to talk us out of it. Statistically, he was right."

HENRY'S DEDUCTIONS

- Never be satisfied. Always reach higher.
- Do what needs to be done—now!
- Understand, anticipate, and satisfy your customers' needs before a competitor does.

Chapter 9

Going Places

Halfway up the uninviting stairway, Bob Johnson almost turned around. "What kind of outfit would work out of a place like *this*?" the former second-baseman in the New York Giants organization asked himself. But having answered an ad in the *Kansas City Star* that cold January day of 1957, he knew Henry Bloch was expecting him. And he could use the extra income to supplement his earnings at the U.S. Post Office and to pay his tuition at Kansas City Kansas Community College.

Bob glanced around the meagerly furnished room at the top of the stairs. There was a receptionist's desk, a waiting area with cheap dinette chairs lined along one wall, and several tax preparer stations that lacked any sense of privacy. "This company couldn't amount to much," he thought. But he felt better after being warmly greeted by, as he says, "a beautiful redhead." It was Marion Bloch, who occasionally helped out at the front desk or in the back, where finished returns were processed.

During the interview, Henry surmised two things: Bob knew taxes, having done returns for family and friends, and clients would like him. Bob was equally impressed with Henry. "I decided that here's the gentleman to tie your wagon to," Bob says. "He's going places." But a month into the job, Henry ordered Bob into his office to meet with him and Dick.

"Why did you charge *$125* for this return?" Henry was upset because the whopping fee for that single return equaled 25 average returns. But in the back of his mind, Henry couldn't help but think that there might be an untapped market for mid-level executives who don't want to pay CPA prices.

"I didn't want to insult the man," Bob replied. The executive had paid a CPA $250 the previous year and was dissatisfied with the service. H and R remained unconvinced. Just as they were about to lecture Bob about the importance of adhering to the pricing schedule, Marion suddenly walked into Henry's office.

"Bob, two gentlemen are here to see you," she said. "The executive who came in yesterday was so impressed with your service that he told his associates to have you prepare their returns." The conversation hastily concluded as Bob excused himself to work on one of the men's taxes.

Henry introduced himself to the other man, offering to do his return so he wouldn't have to wait for Bob. "No, thank you," the man told Henry. "I would prefer to see Mr. Johnson."

Like a Family

Top preparers like Bob were eager to assume a larger role in the firm's burgeoning success. "They wanted to grow with us," Henry says. "It was like a family." During the traditional late-night April 15th party at the main office, it was customary for tax pros, one by one, to make their case in Dick's office to open new markets. "What do you want out of life? What is your ambition?" Dick always asked the budding entrepreneurs.

Henry and Dick didn't wait for Bob to approach them. He was their pick to open the Wichita offices. But Bob countered with three demands. First, he wanted the right to open Los Angeles as soon as the brothers were ready to conquer the West Coast. Second, instead of $500 a month for five months, he needed $800. And third, he insisted on keeping 75 percent of the earnings in Wichita, not the standard 50 percent. The brothers were so impressed by Bob that they acquiesced, and his lucrative contract remained in force for 10 years before the split was cut to 50 percent. When Bob was later offered Los Angeles, he turned Henry down. "My family and I were well situated in Wichita," he says. (When Bob retired after 36 years with H&R Block in Wichita, he returned to his roots as a tax preparer.)

The Blochs needed a strategy so they could reach into rural communities with populations lower than 15,000. It didn't make economic or operational sense to try to manage small, remote towns as company-owned offices. So they fashioned a new type of franchise for their system called a "satellite." The satellite franchisees paid half of their gross revenues to the company in return for advertising, training, and the supplies needed to run the business. In 1959, the first satellite opened in tiny Yates Center, Kansas, located in a county of fewer than 6,000 people. Satellite owners were not merely preparers and business owners; they were Block ambassadors in their communities. The large territorial franchises, such as the state of Oklahoma, also established satellite offices in small towns, which were essentially subfranchises of the parent company.

"In every business and particularly every service business, people are the most valuable asset," Henry always said. "The people who meet our customers face-to-face *are* H&R Block. Our success has always been due to quality, customer-oriented people in our organization." Pat Merriman is such a person.

Pat did taxes on his own in Lubbock and Amarillo, Texas. "It was a kitchen-table business," he says. "Either I went to my clients' house or they came to mine." Wanting to expand in Texas, the brothers found Pat's name in the membership roster of the Lubbock Chamber of Commerce. They wrote him about becoming part of their emerging franchise organization.

Eighteen inches of snow in Kansas City didn't deter Pat from making the trip to learn more. "I stayed at the Netherlands Hotel, where the room rate was $3," he recalls. "I didn't find a bed in my room!

Then I was told that it dropped down from the wall—it was a Murphy bed. A sign on the wall read, 'No Cooking Allowed in Rooms,' yet the hallways reeked of food."

Scoping out the quiet tax office on that late November morning, Pat noticed the peculiar-looking desktops. Just as he determined that they were made out of doors, a voice came out of one of the three private offices: "May I help you?" Dick suddenly appeared and offered the Texan a seat in his plain-looking office. Pat noted countless cigarette burns on the edge of Dick's desk, but that was not his primary concern. He was in town with about a dozen other prospects from different cities for a daylong meeting with Dick and Henry about expanding the Block brand. The meeting took place in the tax office. Dinner followed at the partially furnished house that Dick and Annette had recently purchased. The makeshift dining room table was a large piece of plywood on two sawhorses. A bed sheet served as the tablecloth.

Before leaving for the airport, Dick presented Pat with a franchise contract for Lubbock. Impressed with the brothers and their vision to dot the nation with tax offices, he signed up. And so did the others who came to town for the meeting. "I didn't see any downside to it," Pat says. The agreement allowed franchisees to exclude royalties on the fees paid for returns prepared for their previous clients.

His single Lubbock outlet in 1959 had decent results. "I saw enough in that one office that I opened Amarillo the next season," Pat says. That same year, he, Bob Johnson, and Henry took the Treasury Department's written exam to become enrolled agents. The test score determines who is allowed to represent taxpayers before the Internal Revenue Service. Although each of them passed, the IRS denied them enrolled-agent status because H&R Block was a commercial tax firm that advertised its service. (The IRS eventually allowed commercial preparers to become enrolled agents, although Henry never received a Treasury Card.)

Pat expanded throughout Texas, becoming the biggest franchisee in the Block system. His Lone Star State empire grew even bigger when he later acquired the Oklahoma and southwest Arkansas franchises.

Another star in Block's nascent talent pool was Bill Ross. As a teenager, he dropped out of high school to shovel coal in railway cars. His father had deserted the family during the Great Depression, forcing Bill to become the breadwinner. Required to file a return since he was 16,

Bill taught himself taxes. Later he and a cousin had a small roofing and siding outfit. "The construction business was slow that winter of 1961," Bill says. "So I responded to an H&R Block newspaper ad. Henry interviewed me, asked me a number of tax questions, and hired me to work in the Independence, Missouri, office."

"I fell in love with the darn work," Bill continues. "When I did taxes, my job was to live the customers' financial life. I tried to dig out deductions." Bill's clients appreciated his thoroughness and dedication. But one couple felt sorry for him. The office was swamped the day Bill prepared their return and he didn't have time to eat. "When they came back the following year, they brought me lunch."

Bill was a self-taught jack-of-all-trades and a master of them all. "After my third season, Henry wouldn't let me go back to the construction business," Bill says. From keeping books to installing exhaust fans that rid the tax offices of billowing clouds of cigarette smoke, Bill did it all. He worked closely with Henry and Dick in a variety of capacities during the company's go-go years and well beyond.

As the company's footprint advanced and newer offices matured, revenues and earnings multiplied. But even when the company surpassed the $1 million mark in tax preparation fees in 1961, Henry still wasn't convinced that their string of luck would last. He knew Congress could put them out of business by drastically simplifying the tax code. Or a national company with deep pockets could speedily snatch the market away from them.

In the meantime, he didn't deprive his family of their regular two-week summer vacations on Cape Cod or Martha's Vineyard. "I hope we can have just one more good year," Henry regularly updated Marion during their annual holidays. He took pleasure in treating his family to nice vacations, and he never skimped on food or lodging.

It was fashionable for black limousines to pull up to the prestigious Plaza Hotel on New York's swanky Fifth Avenue across from Central Park. But the Bloch clan garnered its share of stares when, on their way to Cape Cod one summer, the sixsome pulled up to the imposing entrance in Marion's filthy station wagon with its Kansas license plate and a pile of luggage strapped on the roof. "The doorman looked at us like we were from outer space," Henry recalls. "He asked if we were at the right hotel."

Going Public

It was also fashionable for successful private companies to go public in the early 1960s. Henry and Dick considered the idea as a way to diversify their personal holdings and raise capital to accelerate office expansion. Besides reducing their share of ownership in the company, a stock offering would require them to report on business results to investors, who would have a say in how the company is run.

In 1961, they lined up a lawyer and an underwriter to take the company public. And they retained an accounting firm to produce audited financial statements. In the middle of the audit, however, the accountants failed to show up for work. Henry phoned the firm: "Your people aren't here today. Is there a problem?"

"Yes," the lead accountant replied. "Our headquarters ordered us to suspend the audit because your company is competing with CPAs." When other accounting firms declined to perform the audit for the same reason, the law firm and underwriter backed out. Henry was stunned and disappointed.

After the abandoned underwriting, groups of accountants and lawyers continued to complain about unfair competition. They grumbled that the unregulated tax firm charging absurdly low prices was advertising its service, which CPAs and attorneys were prohibited from doing. Lawsuits aimed at preventing commercial tax preparers from advertising failed. But Henry had a lingering worry that if states enacted legislation requiring professional tax preparers to be either CPAs or lawyers, H&R Block's future could be jeopardized.

Soon after the failed offering, Ken Baum, a high-school classmate of Marion's and the president of the investment firm George K. Baum & Company, called on the brothers.

"I'd like to take you public," he told them. "But we would go about it in a different way."

Ken imagined forming a separate company out of the tax offices in the Midwest. "Take public only this subset of offices, not the entire office network," he advocated. But that was only half the plan. In exchange for stock, the brothers would gradually sell the remaining tax offices, once they were in the black, to the public company. Henry

H. & R. BLOCK CO. CONVENTION • Salt Lake City, Utah • 1962

Henry and Richard (first row, center) with Block's senior field managers and major franchisees in 1962

and Dick took a liking to Ken's idea. So Ken scouted out a lawyer and accounting firm willing to take the much smaller entity public.

The initial board of directors for the new company included Henry, Dick, Ken, and the local attorney who worked on the public offering, Marvin Rich. The 75,000-share offering generated $4 per share. As planned, the brothers didn't pocket the $300,000 cash infusion; they used it to expand their network. And as soon as additional states turned a profit, the public company purchased the entities from the brothers.

Just when the plan's execution seemed to be going flawlessly, Henry and Dick received a letter from the Securities and Exchange Commission. It was initiating an investigation into the curious transactions between the founders and the public company. The letter shook Henry. He immediately called Ken, who recommended that they retain Ed Smith, a top Kansas City attorney, to handle the case. After a thorough examination, the SEC closed its file, concluding that neither the public company nor the brothers had done anything wrong. Henry was relieved to put the distraction behind them.

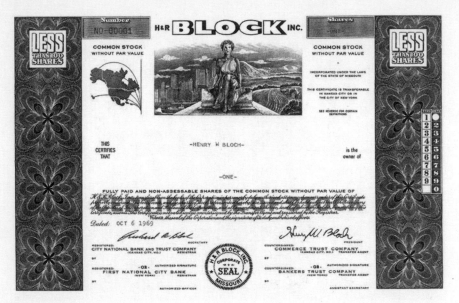

When H&R Block went public in 1962, the first stock certificate was issued to Henry

The Blochs were so impressed with Ed's legal and business acumen that they routinely engaged him to tackle the thorniest of their growing company's legal matters. Eventually they invited him to join their board of directors. Ed was more than willing to accept Block stock in lieu of cash as payment for his services. But the brothers chose to pay him in cash.

As it turned out, the previous year's abandoned public offering worked to Henry and Dick's advantage for two reasons. First, the company's value was considerably higher a year later. Second, the founders ended up selling a much smaller portion of their total holdings, allowing them to retain greater ownership in their mushrooming business.

In 1963, the thriving tax firm prepared its one-millionth return. Its main tax office on Main Street was busting at the seams. The brothers constructed a basic, 7,000-square-foot, concrete-block building down the street. The 200-person headquarters housed its flagship tax office in which annual shareholders' meetings were held. A print shop and supply warehouse occupied the basement. Henry and Dick had adjacent offices on the north side overlooking the parking lot.

Two "firsts" occurred the following year. One was the establishment of a franchise in Calgary, representing the first Block office outside the United States. The company also sued its New York City franchise, charging unscrupulous practices relating to pricing and advertising. Two years later, Block agreed to settle the suit by paying more than $1 million for the franchise that it had originally sold for a mere $10,000.

The Bloch brothers made a perfect team. While Henry focused on details and execution, Dick concentrated on the big picture and big ideas. Henry's management style could be described as deliberate, thoughtful, and considerate. Dick was swift, energetic, and tough. While Henry preferred documentation, Dick's files were mostly in his head. He would say, "My word is my bond."

The two brothers led the company together. Henry finally told Dick, "If we continue to jointly make every decision, we won't get anything done." They carved up the responsibilities, agreeing that each of them could veto any decision the other made. And in the event of a veto, they agreed to never hold hard feelings toward each other. They had always swapped titles annually. When Henry was President and Treasurer, Dick was Vice President and Secretary. But in 1964, Dick permanently took the post of Chairman of the Board, and Henry kept the title of President.

The company benefited from the founders' distinct personas. They were down-to-earth businessmen, passionate about their work and their cigars. Dick preferred the fat ones and Henry the thin. Both were tight with a dollar, although Dick was the more frugal. Morton Sosland, who joined the company's board in 1963, says, "Dick was as penurious a person as God has ever made."

Once Dick phoned the Topeka office and got a recorded message. "Do you realize how much it would cost if we put answering machines in every office?" he exclaimed.

Defending their unyielding frugality, Henry says, "We had to watch expenses closely because we didn't charge much for our service."

The brothers also watched their salaries. For years, the two tax titans earned $32,000 apiece. "The board tried repeatedly to give us a raise, but we turned them down," Henry says. "We figured that if the company reports higher earnings, all shareholders, including the two of us, would benefit."

HENRY'S DEDUCTIONS

- People are the most important asset in your business. Listen to them, help them, empower them, and reward them when they perform well.
- Dedicate yourself to the things you are passionate about.
- If you work hard and try to do what's right, things usually turn out for the best.

Chapter 10

Learning to Soar

To get the word out about their tax service, the brothers relied on newspaper advertising and window signs. Radio and television were later added to the mix. Bob Johnson, manager of Block's Wichita operation, was one of the first to test TV ads. "The Kansas City office furnished a script," he recalls, "and I read it on the air."

Initially the company sponsored the weather segment of local 10 o'clock evening news broadcasts. The rationale was simple: The average TV viewer is interested in knowing about the next day's weather. "It worked—and it worked sensationally," Dick wrote in his memoirs.

After the company's stock went public, a securities analyst urged Henry and Dick to hire a Madison Avenue ad agency. They complied, and it was a good thing they did. Picking former NBC anchorman John Cameron Swayze as their television spokesman boosted the company's national image. Bill Ross, who played the role of a tax preparer in some of the commercials, remembers an outtake: "Swayze was supposed to point at a map of the United States and say, 'We've got an office near you.' He jokingly added, 'And if we don't, then move!'" In another outtake, Henry remembers Swayze saying, "They have offices all over the damn place."

The TV messages underscored Block's expertise, low prices, convenience, free year-round assistance, and a guarantee to pay any penalty and interest if the company made a mistake. At the end of each ad, Swayze pledged, "You'll be glad you got together."

Once when Swayze was in town filming commercials, Henry invited him over to the house for dinner.

"Can I help you?" Henry asked the bald-headed stranger who rang the doorbell that evening. The man introduced himself as Swayze. "I didn't recognize him," an embarrassed Henry says. "He wasn't wearing his toupee."

Block didn't retain a public relations firm but, as Henry says, "We've always had the best PR agency in the world—the United States Congress. Politicians are always talking about changing the tax laws, which creates taxpayer anxiety and confusion. Continued tinkering with the tax code has almost always resulted in increased complexity."

Little Details

In 1964, H&R Block's 500,000 clients drank 30 tons of coffee, and their children sucked on 50,000 lollipops. The company ran through 10 million sheets of paper, 2,500 refillable mechanical pencils, 432,000 inches of lead, and 18 million staples.

"The whole business is nothing but little details," Henry once said. "We have been trying to find a pencil constructed so the lead won't break while the preparer is with the customer. We reworked the tax forms to simplify their filling out. We can't change page one, but we have arranged other schedules so they can be filled out faster and easier and do double duty for federal and state returns. We've worked out a desk pad that has the tax tables—so while the preparer is doing his figuring, he doesn't have to reach for a tax book."[1]

In 1965, the firm prepared one million returns in a single season. The brothers decided to stop franchising in cities with a population over 50,000 because company-owned offices were more profitable than franchises. And Block could now afford the up-front investment to open scores of new offices. But even as the balance sheet grew stronger, Henry and Dick relentlessly preached and modeled thriftiness. As Henry said, "We scrimped and saved so that we didn't have to raise prices." True to form, they didn't raise them.

The Blochs' top priority was not to grow profits; it was to grow the number of customers. "Our goal is to prepare 10 percent of the nation's returns," Henry declared that same year. And as they divulged in their annual report to shareholders, "Every facet of our business is secondary to customer satisfaction."

There was another reason why the brothers kept expenses low. "We refused to borrow money," Henry says.

By focusing on high customer approval ratings and low operating expenses, meteoric revenue growth followed. Earnings escalated at rates hovering 50 percent a year. The share price followed suit. Henry heard about an investor in the United Kingdom who had the company's name

Dick and Henry in H&R
Block's main tax office in
Kansas City

tiled in the bottom of his brand new swimming pool, which was paid for with gains on Block stock. The two founders owned 84 percent of the company's stock until 1966, when they reduced their combined ownership to 55 percent. Strong growth persisted as the company filed a record 3 percent of all U.S. returns. That year, the television commercials featuring John Cameron Swayze were produced in color.

Each tax season, the brothers inspected as much of their far-flung network as they could. Henry took turns bringing his children on trips, even if it meant they missed a few days of school.

"I think they benefited from the experience," Henry says, "and it gave me an excuse not to stay out too late with our local managers."

Dick, who loved to fly, bought a single-engine plane that he piloted himself when he dropped in on hard-to-get-to locations, often unannounced. Bill Ross remembers being the sole passenger on a trip to Rockford, Illinois, and Davenport, Iowa.

"The darn thing stalled out and died in mid-air!" he recalls. "Dick frantically pushed and pulled levers and turned knobs. Finally he got it started up before we hit anything." After that one spine-chilling experience, Bill refused to fly again with Dick.

As the business soared, the brothers had to create additional layers of management. Bill became a vice president and took responsibility for a third of the U.S. operation. Along with Henry and Dick, he also conducted training for tax preparers who were promoted to city managers.

"They came from all kinds of backgrounds," Bill explains. The man who opened San Diego, for example, was a lather (a construction worker who installs boards that support plaster coatings). The Chicago manager had been a Packard car salesman, and the North Dakota operator was a farmer. "We taught them everything—how to hire, run ads, keep the books, locate offices, and manage."

Almost every employee, including seasonal tax preparers, was awarded stock options. Tax pros couldn't exercise the options unless they returned the following tax season, making them an excellent retention tool.

"One of the side benefits of the stock option plan was the pride of ownership it instilled in many employees," Dick wrote in his memoirs. He knew a receptionist in Mission, Kansas, who owned 25 shares and "ran the office like it was her own ball game." When tax preparers went through a roll of adding machine paper, she made them use the reverse side. "She wanted those dividends to grow."

Joe Janco was 21 years old when he started checking tax returns in Lawrence, Massachusetts. He remembers coming to Kansas City for management training. "You could ask Henry anything," he says. "He trusted us and appreciated what we were doing for our clients. When he admitted that headquarters didn't have all the answers, he had my loyalty from that point on. If he had told me to jump off a bridge, I would have done it."

Joe thought this was going to be a stepping-stone to another career, but he fell in love with the business. "As I got into management, I found that the people I worked with weren't there just to make money," he says. "They were there to help people. It got in my blood, and I was hooked. It was so much more than a job."

The Best Ideas

Henry knew that the best ideas came from the folks in the field. One brainstorm was the pinned map. Color-coded by office, pins were stuck in a city map according to the neighborhoods where the clients lived. Knowing that most consumers wouldn't travel more than two miles to a tax office, managers used the data to determine where to relocate outlets or open new ones.

Another idea from the field was to retain tax offices all year long. Leasing offices for four months gave the impression of a fly-by-night business; year-round locations, even if they weren't open during the entire off-season, created a sense of permanency. The inspiration to start Executive Tax Service, later relabeled H&R Block Premium, also came from the field. Designed to attract higher-income taxpayers, these more upscale offices featured private offices for preparers and clients, nicer furnishings, and higher fees.

National operations meetings with field managers and franchisees spawned these and countless other ideas. "We got together every year and discussed every element of the business. We set policy and procedure," Pat Merriman recalls. "Our meeting in New Orleans lasted 10 days. I never got out early enough to go to Bourbon Street."

One topic that was always discussed at national operations meetings was attracting and hiring well-trained tax preparers. With approximately 40 percent of clients coming in during the first two weeks of April, adequate staffing was essential. The company's tax schools charged $40 tuition for a 72-hour course lasting eight weeks. Graduates who worked a full season were refunded the tuition. In 1967, 10,000 students enrolled in the course, and over half were hired. That same year, Collier Books published the *H&R Block Income Tax Workbook* at a price of $1.95. The company refunded the amount to purchasers who were unable to complete their return using the book, provided they allowed a Block office to do their taxes.

In 1969, the company opened its first office in New Zealand, and its over-the-counter stock moved over to the New York Stock Exchange. The high-performing shares had split four times in four years. Its dividend increased for the seventh consecutive year. According to Henry, anyone who had invested $12,000 in 1962 would be worth over $1 million in 1969. The company was on a roll. A year later, the firm's vast web of over 4,000 locations filed almost 10 percent of U.S. returns. And in 1971, the office network expanded to Australia and towns near U.S. military bases in Germany. *Forbes* listed H&R Block as the nation's 372nd largest company in terms of market value.

The *Forbes* listing seemed to mitigate a downbeat if not downright poisonous assessment of the company in a widely-read business publication. "The reporter wrote that Block stock wasn't worth the paper it was printed on," Henry recalls. "It was yellow journalism." Henry met with the editor, who offered to print a retort if Henry cared to write one. But he and the board decided it was best to put the matter behind them.

Even as the small business developed into a big business, it still felt like a family business. As *Newsweek* put it, "One key to the Blochs' success is a folksy, personalized approach to customers, who frequently view Internal Revenue as a dread monolith. Free coffee is served to everybody—they figure 10 million cups this year—and crayons and coloring books are provided for those who drag their kids along."[2]

The Blochs' friendly and informal approach to customers didn't prevent local and regional competitors from popping up, aiming to imitate the brothers' success. In some cases, the competition was in the form of ex-Block employees striking out on their own. But still there was no organized national competition.

"There is no second," Henry declared in 1970. To emphasize the point, he curved his index finger to within a smidgen of his thumb and declared, "We're only this big—and still there is no second."[3]

H&R Block was the industry leader—not only in size but also in morals. Bill Ross, who started as a part-time preparer and never left, explains: "What kept me going were the company's strong ethical roots. Henry insisted that everyone treat the customers right, and he stood behind what he promised."

Decades after he signed on as a seasonal employee, Joe Janco agrees. "The founders had a vision that if you are taking care of the clients, then you are also taking care of the stockholders and the employees."

"There are simple things that insure a successful operation," Henry lectured the field managers. His top ten were: (1) work hard, (2) be honest, (3) preach courtesy, (4) keep your word, (5) be enthusiastic, (6) seek improvement and never be satisfied, (7) know and understand the policy and procedure book, (8) know income taxes, (9) prepare reports on time, and (10) honor each client. He encouraged managers to discard bad habits and not postpone solving problems. "It is never too late to change from wrong to right. And remember, the business is made up of lots of details, each being the most important."

HENRY'S DEDUCTIONS

- First and foremost, make decisions with your customers in mind.
- Give others credit. You'll get more in return.
- If the sign in your window is crooked, then other things in your office are wrong.

Chapter 11

Setbacks and Comebacks

Henry felt confident. The firm had achieved 16 straight years of astonishing growth. The 1971 tax season had been the best yet. He began receiving invitations to join boards of local nonprofit and civic organizations and, feeling a moral obligation to give back to his community, he accepted them. But his top priorities remained his family and his business.

The brothers always included a letter in the annual report that candidly assessed the previous tax season and envisaged the next one. Articulating an upbeat outlook was routine, and their optimism always bore out. "We look forward with confidence and sincere optimism," they wrote shareholders in anticipation of 1972.

The Blochs employed the same winning formula that had worked so successfully each preceding year: Enlarge the retail footprint, provide quality service, keep costs and prices low, and promote the brand.

As usual, the offices expected another influx of taxpayers, bringing about increased revenues and earnings. H&R Block had become to taxes what Timex was to watches and Kodak was to film. Johnny Carson cracked jokes about the company in his monologues, referring to the firm as H&R Schlock or H&R Goniff. Henry even appeared as a guest on the popular *Tonight Show*.

But the 1972 tax season was no laughing matter. The assault started when the IRS commissioner announced to over 75 million taxpayers on the cover of the Form 1040 packet that more than 30 million of them could prepare their own returns. He also said that if outside help were sought, taxpayers should be wary of certain commercial preparers. Henry was insulted by the commissioner's remarks.

That was just the beginning. During the filing season, the IRS launched an investigation directed at fraudulent preparers. But the publicity surrounding the investigation affected the public's trust in all commercial tax preparation firms, regardless of quality.

Henry recalls that the commissioner added to the problem by suggesting that Form 1040 was so simple that fifth graders could complete it. Newspapers followed up with accounts of fifth graders who were tested to determine if they were up to the task. "They couldn't do it," Henry recalls. But the damage to the industry was done.

To make matters worse, the IRS offered and promoted free taxpayer assistance. Henry publicly raised questions about the program, suggesting that the world's largest collection agency should focus its resources on collections. "A dollar spent in auditing taxpayers yields $10 in revenue," he said. In addition, independent accounts suggested that the IRS didn't always provide accurate assistance.

Many taxpayers, who were paying out hundreds of millions of dollars annually to professional preparers, could deduct these fees on their Form 1040s. The tax deductions essentially reduced the amount collected by the U.S. Treasury. Henry conjectured that the campaign to discourage taxpayers from using commercial preparers may have been partially motivated by the government putting its own financial interests over the taxpayers' wellbeing.

The Federal Trade Commission got into the tussle by filing a complaint against H&R Block. The FTC stated that there was an implication that Block, which promised to accompany clients on IRS audits, would act as the taxpayers' legal counsel. The FTC also argued that the company's guarantee to pay penalties or interest charges in the event of an error sounded as if it would pay additional taxes that were owed. The agency further charged that Block had used confidential information in soliciting its customers for other financial products. The latter claim was true. Block had used client information to market insurance products—until a federal law was passed forbidding such practices. As Henry says, "It burned us up because we already had stopped it." To put the FTC matter to bed and avoid more negative publicity, the company signed a consent decree with the FTC, agreeing to cease actions without admitting having taken part in illegal acts.

Even tax reform, which typically benefited the industry, dealt an unusual blow in 1972. By raising the minimum level of income required for filing a return, Congress removed some of the lowest wage earners from the tax rolls. "These were our kind of people," Henry says. "We underestimated the impact of the change on the market. We shouldn't have expanded."

In the face of the assaults, Block's board urged Henry to meet with Johnnie Walters, the IRS commissioner. Mr. Walters told Henry that his agency's attacks on the industry would help reputable firms such as H&R Block. "I thought to myself, 'With friends like that, who needs enemies?'" Henry recalls. The commissioner prophesized that shoddy operators would be forced to close their doors and reputable firms would wind up stronger. Henry remained skeptical.

In addition to attacks on the industry and a reduction in the tax rolls, Block's advertising was ineffective. Its newly hired ad agency had developed witty, if not comical, commercials for 1972 that made light of taxes. As amusing as the ads were, they didn't drive taxpayers into the offices. "We learned an expensive lesson," Henry says. "Taxpayers don't joke around when it comes to dealing with the IRS." Ironically, the campaign won the exalted "Clio" for the best national campaign of the year.

When the dreadful tax season drew to a close, so did the company's string of earnings increases. Net income declined 34 percent. Block's stock price plummeted from $42 to $9 a share.

The Aftermath

Henry grew concerned about the growth prospects for the commercial tax industry. He and Dick decided that the company should branch out beyond taxes. If successful businesses operating in other industries could be developed or acquired, they figured, Block would become less dependent on tax preparation.

The brothers made their first diversification move in 1972. They acquired a small company called Consumer Communications Services Corporation, based in Columbus, Ohio. CCSC competed with the U.S. Postal Service by distributing advertising materials door-to-door via a unique system of "mailmaids."

Diversifying seemed like a smart, defensive move at the time because the government's assault on storefront tax preparers didn't stop when the tax season came to an end. Some members of Congress made the case that consumers need protection from abusive tax preparation services. Henry agreed. He testified before the House Ways and Means Committee and the Senate Finance Committee, advocating legislation to regulate the industry. "We favor registration for anyone who prepares more than ten income tax returns a year for a fee," he said. Henry also recommended a "standard of competence" and "some reasonable control of advertising practices."

Block responded to the arduous market conditions in other ways. Its board of directors began holding monthly meetings. Five hundred storefronts were shuttered, and 20 percent of the field management team was laid off. Executive vice president Jerry Grossman, who was a cousin of Marion's, a fraternity brother of Henry's, and a six-year veteran of the company, shouldered additional operational responsibilities. He instituted a mystery-shopping program to formally measure the quality of Block's service. (Mystery shoppers are trained to report back to the company what they experience in a retailer's store.) He appointed franchisees to a satellite council to thrash out new ideas and improve communications with the franchisor.

The management shake-up was the first for the company. Initiating the cuts was an unpleasant task for Henry, but he knew it was necessary. A few employees, including Ken Treat, benefited from the cutback. He was promoted from city manager to regional director in Chicago.

Initially hired by Bob Johnson as a tax preparer in Wichita, Kansas, Ken remembers the aftermath of the 1972 tax season. "It was like getting hit in the stomach and having all the air taken out of your lungs," he says. "All of the regional directors got together in Kansas City that fall. We took a notch out of our belt and reacted. We became a closer family."

Before the 1973 tax season, senior management searched for a new advertising agency. They selected BBD&O, a leading New York firm. Jim Jordan, the group's creative genius, was behind such slogans as "Ring around the collar!" and "Us Tareyton smokers would rather fight than switch!" Jim told Henry, "The best person to sell the service is the one whose name is on the door." The "17 Reasons" advertising campaign was born, making Henry an instant national celebrity. In each spot he stressed why taxpayers should go to H&R Block. "Reason 14.

Henry began pitching his
"17 Reasons" in 1973

We're human, and once in a great while we make a mistake. But if our error means you must pay additional tax, you pay only the tax. We pay any interest or penalty. We stand behind our work."

Henry was an outstanding pitchman. He radiated trust. As *Time* reported, Henry "looks like a small-town tooth driller. He is a direct, plain-spoken Midwesterner in a brown suit and brown shoes, the type of fellow for whom the word unpretentious was invented."[1] The campaign ran for 10 straight tax seasons. It didn't win a Clio, but brand awareness and consumer attitudes toward the company reached new highs.

Just as the firm realigned and reinvigorated itself, the IRS publicized results of an analysis of professionally prepared tax returns. The data showed that *half* of the paid returns in their sample displayed careless errors, inaccuracies, or cheating. Henry was appalled by the report. It gave the industry another black eye.

According to one newspaper account, "a severe shaking out is in prospect for professional tax preparers."[2] It was now beginning to appear that Commissioner Walters' prediction was correct—the industry would be cleaned up. But would Block emerge stronger or weaker?

The commissioner addressed this question in a written response to Henry two weeks after the 1973 tax season. "It seems increasingly clear to me, as I leave office, that the long term, and indeed the short term, interests of the legitimate returns preparation industry will be served well by the efforts of the Internal Revenue Service to drive the fly-by-night and the inept from the field. I believe you yourself, and the industry you represent, are coming to this same view. In this light, therefore, there is really no conflict between us."

"The commissioner was right," Henry says. "Shady operators closed their doors. We bounced back in 1973."

Improved marketing and major cost-cutting initiatives, including a reduction in the number of offices by 6 percent, helped boost earnings 54 percent. Not only was new client growth strong, but the number of returning customers reached a record 78 percent. Henry and Dick finally yielded to inflationary pressures. For the first time ever, they raised prices. The average charge was about $13.

For some time Henry and Dick had wanted to open tax offices in the nation's largest department store chain. They thought the high-traffic locations would generate new tax customers. Sears was interested, but insisted that the kiosks be branded with its company identification. After the brothers refused, the leading retailer and the leading tax preparer eventually compromised, settling on Sears Income Tax Service by H&R Block. A test of 147 locations in 1973 was the start of a beautiful marriage. As Henry said, "It's like two and two equals five." The company rolled out the Sears relationship the following year, and it began contemplating partnerships with other retailers.

Distractions

Despite the dramatic comeback, Henry still worried about the firm's long-term growth prospects. "Our company is maturing. If we stay exclusively in tax preparation in the next 10 years, we will show a drastically lower rate of increase," he told *BusinessWeek*. "I want the growth to keep going up."[3] The board agreed with Henry, and it authorized an active diversification program. Henry and Dick began to pursue new frontiers just as their first acquisition was going awry.

As one report stated, "The Blochs first stuck their toes into diversification waters in 1972 and found it a bit chilly. They bought an outfit called Consumer Communications Service Corp., which employed mostly housewives to distribute plastic bags filled with promotional materials and samples. By last year, it provided less than 4 percent of the company's revenues, and it is now retreating from almost half the cities it serves."[4]

But instead of redoubling its diversification efforts, senior management was distracted by antitrust lawsuits and other franchise issues. When the original contracts for the large territorial franchises were conceived, nobody dreamed that the business would become so successful or valuable. The early agreements were for a period of only four years, automatically renewable for successive one-year periods—unless cancelled. In 1964, the company agreed it would not cancel the contracts without reasonable cause. But that concession didn't go far enough to satisfy the franchisees' concerns. So Henry agreed to go a step further in 1973, granting time to cure problems to avoid termination.[5]

The rapport between management and the large franchisees recovered as the issues were resolved.

On rare occasions, the rapport between Henry and Dick also needed attention. And who better to put an end to a squabble between siblings than their mother.

"Drop whatever you're doing and come right over to the house!" Horty demanded.

"Mom always found out when Dick and I had an argument," Henry says. One of them told her, or she found out during daily phone calls with her daughters-in-law. It became a familiar routine; her sons jogged up the steep concrete steps leading to the front door of the two-story Spanish-style house with a yellow stucco exterior, red tile roof, and one-car garage. They marched upstairs to her small sitting room, where she held court.

"Now, what's wrong?" Horty would ask one of her sons.

"What's your version of it?" she inquired of the other.

"By the time we were finished, everything was patched up," Henry says.

Horty taught her sons to confront business problems head-on. Some of the obstacles were unexpected.

One morning Dick walked into Henry's office and sat down across from his desk. With a somber look, he told Henry that that he had decided to cut back. Dick wanted to concentrate solely on operations outside of North America, which primarily comprised Australia and New Zealand. "He and Annette loved to travel," Henry says.

"I was incapable of doing anything halfway," Dick wrote in his memoirs. "I wanted to take life a little easier. I was able to cut back from probably 70 hours a week to an average of 40 hours."

Henry wasn't happy with his partner's decision. "Dick was as responsible for the success of H&R Block as I was," Henry says. "I wasn't sure how I would do without him." But perhaps Dick was better suited for an entrepreneurial role in an emerging business than an executive role in a large organization.

"When the company was smaller, Dick had rapport with the people in the tax offices," Dick's wife Annette says. "He loved that. But as the company got much bigger, it also got more impersonal. That saddened Dick." As he phased out of management, Dick too had concerns about how Henry and the maturing company he was leaving behind would make out.

The board promptly bestowed the new title of Chief Executive Officer on Henry. Jerry Grossman became Chief Operating Officer, and Dick remained chairman of the board.

Block continued to flourish under Henry's leadership. After multiple stock splits, one share of stock originally issued in 1962 was worth fifteen shares in 1974. He oversaw an experienced field team of four divisional directors, 33 regional directors, and 500 managers, who in turn oversaw the company's vast office network. Although most of the fly-by-night operators had been weeded out, reputable competitors, mainly regional and local in scope, sprang up. The bigger outfits included Tax Corporation of America, Beneficial Finance, and Mister Tax. Yet no one was close to Block's size. As Henry reminded shareholders, "We dominate the income tax preparation industry and remain the unchallenged leader in our field."

The company's 7,000 offices, 10 percent of which were located in Sears and other department stores, topped the $100 million mark in fees. Over 49,000 students enrolled in the company's tax courses. Two years later, the customer count surpassed ten million, even as

A typical H&R Block office in the early 1970s

annual price hikes were implemented to offset spiraling inflation. But the company's market share seemed to hit a ceiling at 10 percent as the IRS's simplified Short Form proliferated.

Henry's son, Tom, signed on with the company after graduating from college in 1976. One of his first tasks was to help automate the tax preparation process. It was becoming apparent that doing tax returns on computers would enhance quality and produce economic benefits, assuming the firm's vast seasonal workforce would embrace the technology.

That same year, Henry and Marion began to collect works of art by French Impressionist masters. Their first acquisition was a small Renoir, called *Woman Leaning on her Elbows*, which they purchased from a New York gallery. They enjoyed the painting so much that they bought a second Renoir months later, followed by a powerful portrait by Toulouse-Lautrec. Over time, their collection would grow in both size and stature.

A Dreadful Diagnosis

Life seemed to come to an abrupt standstill for the Richard Bloch family. In 1978, Dick was diagnosed with lung cancer.

"I had been a heavy cigarette smoker, some two to three packs a day," Dick wrote. "On the day the Surgeon General's report on cigarettes came out [in 1964], I was staying in a motel room in San Francisco with our Sacramento manager." Both of them decided to immediately give up cigarettes. "I was climbing the walls. I could not take the pressure of the tax season and give up smoking simultaneously. Since the report stated that five cigars a day would not hurt, I rationalized my way into smoking five cheap, junky, plastic-tipped cigars. Most of the time I would just chew on the tips without having the cigar lit. But I not only burned holes in all my shirts and slacks, I know, unintentionally, that I inhaled."

A doctor told Dick his lung cancer was inoperable and that he should get his estate in order. "My feelings at that moment were of total disbelief," Dick wrote. "I was a healthy, happy, fifty-two-year-old man, and things like this always happened to the other guy." Dick didn't accept the doctor's prognosis—nor did Henry.

"I did some research and found an exceptional cancer treatment program at MD Anderson," Henry says. Part of the University of Texas, MD Anderson is recognized as one of the premier cancer centers in the world. Dick went there for treatment.

During his darkest hours, Dick vowed that if he defeated the disease, he would devote his life to helping others beat cancer. "Two years later, the doctors told me I was totally cured," he wrote. "I have no more chance of a recurrence of lung cancer than anyone else on the street."

Dick kept his promise, establishing the R.A. Bloch Cancer Foundation and the Cancer Hotline to help individuals with the illness. He and Annette developed a program to provide free multidisciplinary second opinions, and they sponsored an annual Cancer Survivors Rally. The couple wrote three books about fighting cancer. And through their foundation they provided funding for the creation of Cancer Survivors Parks throughout North America. One of them is located near the MD Anderson Medical Center in downtown Houston.

"After he was cured, Dick told me that he would always sit in the smoking section of airplanes," Henry says. "He figured it meant one less person could smoke."

With a track record of cooking up tremendous ideas, Dick concocted a new one—to form a national network of cancer information. The concept was put into action when the National Cancer Institute launched a web site about treating every type and stage of cancer. To honor his efforts, the government named the building in Bethesda, Maryland, the R.A. Bloch International Cancer Information Center. President Reagan tapped Dick to serve on the National Cancer Advisory Board.

Dick approached the war against cancer as vigorously as he had approached building H&R Block. And his efforts were equally successful. "I often run into people who tell me that my brother saved their life," Henry says.

"There is no such thing as false hope for a cancer patient," Dick said. He personally proved the power of positive thinking—twice. Following his successful battle with lung cancer, he confronted colon cancer. Again, he beat the disease.

While Dick worked tirelessly to improve the odds of those stricken with cancer, Henry continued his efforts to diversify the company. But five years after sketching out his intentions to expand, it was still slow going. "Someone had told me that two out of three acquisitions fail," Henry says. After making a mistake the first time with the purchase of CCSC, he didn't want to be disappointed again.

Henry's Deductions

- Loathe complacency. True winners retain their competitive edge.
- Adversity creates opportunity.
- Great companies have one thing in common—great people.

Chapter 12

Heartbroken

"We're making conscious efforts to become a broad-based company by entering other service-oriented industries," Henry updated shareholders in 1979.

In an interview with the *Wall Street Journal*, he was more specific: "We're looking for acquisitions in service industries, such as specialized computer services and insurance. Ideally we'd like to make an acquisition about every nine months, and we're looking for good, going concerns." He wasn't looking for turnarounds.[1]

Humorist and columnist Art Buchwald offered Henry some advice. "Have you ever considered going into the marriage counseling business?" he wrote. "Next to the tax business, I imagine it is the one that people are most interested in. It would keep your offices going 12 months a year. The same people who do the taxes would do the counseling."

An article in *Forbes* presented a more pragmatic view.

> Henry Bloch has a problem. H&R Block, his 26-year-old firm, has offices in every U.S. city with a population of over 5,000,

and the company prepares 1 out of every 10 federal returns. But with that big a base, new business hardly comes easy. Already, annual growth is down to 11 percent—less than half what it was a decade ago. What's more, there is a troubling trend: Many taxpayers are shifting to the Internal Revenue Service's short form that can be done at home.[2]

Henry finally bit the bullet. He made three diversification moves in three years. First, he bought Personnel Pool of America, a privately owned company headquartered in Ft. Lauderdale, Florida, for $22.5 million. PPA operated 216 temporary help offices, most of which were franchised.

Next, Block paid $23 million to acquire CompuServe, a provider of remote computer services, primarily on a time-sharing basis. "CompuServe is an attractive company because of its highly efficient telecommunications network and library of software packages, which provide sophisticated solutions to business problems," Henry stated after the transaction. "Although synergy between CompuServe's computer technology and H&R Block's tax preparation business was not a primary consideration for the acquisition, we nevertheless expect to benefit from CompuServe's considerable computer knowledge and experience."

A month later, Block created a new subsidiary called Block Management Company. BMC provided marketing and administrative services to Hyatt Legal Clinics, headquartered in Cleveland and operating nine offices in Ohio. Hyatt offered a limited menu of legal services to individuals, including domestic relations, wills, bankruptcy, and probate. As founder Joel Hyatt put it, "What Block did for income tax preparation, we are trying to do for legal services." An initial consultation cost $15, an uncontested divorce was $250, and wills were delivered for $45.[3]

"We saw a similarity in this with our tax services," Henry explained. "Both are designed to make professional services more available to the public. The legal clinics, of course, are designed to make inexpensive attorneys available to people who might need a lawyer but don't believe they can afford one."[4]

But how did the tax man plan to oversee three new businesses that were completely unrelated to tax preparation? "My philosophy was to live and let live," Henry says. "Our subsidiaries formed their own boards of directors. We developed a list of reporting guidelines that gave the parent company the least amount of control but the necessary amount to achieve a level of comfort that was required by a publicly held company."

Stock analysts applauded Henry's efforts to put the company's excess cash to work. As one observer noted, "Finally, H&R are putting some new chips on the old Block. And not a moment too soon, as far as Wall Street is concerned."[5]

But one of the old chips was growing stale. After continually reporting disappointing results, CCSC, the company's first acquisition, was sold.

Overall, the new acquisitions flourished, taking advantage of Block's significant cash reserves and quasi self-governing approach. Hyatt relocated its headquarters to Kansas City and expanded aggressively. PPA also enlarged its North American footprint. But CompuServe made the boldest move of all. Jeff Wilkins, its CEO, was among the first to seize on the idea that home computers would eventually become as commonplace as television sets. Acting on intuition, Jeff repositioned CompuServe as an information service provider for home computer users. As one columnist noted, "CompuServe served as both a lonely hearts club for early online users and as an incubator of online commerce more than a decade before the web was invented."[6] But the online service wasn't cheap; users paid 10 cents a minute.

While Wall Street focused on Block's diversification efforts and particularly CompuServe's makeover, the core tax business continued to dominate its market. In 1981, Block had 8,000 offices, 43,000 seasonal workers, and over 10 million clients. Its closest competitor had merely 250,000 clients.

"We had one of the strongest balance sheets on the New York Stock Exchange," Henry says. But success didn't change Henry, nor did it diminish his resolve to make his company larger and stronger.

"Henry Bloch has maintained a down-to-earth, avuncular style even into the loftiest of tax brackets," *Money* magazine wrote in 1981.[7]

For Dick, helping others battle cancer represented a loftier calling. It had become his new passion, and Henry respected Dick's commitment. In 1982, Dick elected to make a break with the company, selling virtually all of his Block stock in a public offering. He also retired as chairman of the board.

America's tax man

"I hated to separate myself from the institution I helped start and bring up, but I feel it was well worthwhile," Dick wrote. "My father said that once you have three meals a day, you better do something for the next guy." Tom Bloch, who was now running the tax operations, filled the board vacancy.

CompuServe's early gamble on the home information marketplace paid off. By 1984, it owned half of the online market, which was still in its infancy. One year later, its subscriber base grew from 120,000 to 200,000.

Hyatt Legal Clinics operated a network of 120 offices, but the business underperformed. It was a drain on Block's resources. Colocating with tax offices didn't lead to an expected influx of law clients. Henry finally pulled the plug. It was a difficult decision to put the business on the sales block because he had been convinced that the need for low-cost legal services was as compelling as the need for low-cost tax services.

Before the sale closed, Block paid $35 million for Kansas City-based Path Management Industries, the largest marketer of one-day business skills seminars. It offered programs for mid-level managers on such topics as time management, customer service, and negotiation.

In 1986, the core tax business benefited from a technological breakthrough. In a limited test, tax returns were electronically filed from its own offices to the IRS. This was significant because it enabled Block to offer refund anticipation loans through a bank, providing customers with an advance against their tax refund in a matter of days. Henry wasn't a big fan of the loan product, but he recognized that many consumers wanted or needed immediate access to their refund amount. The product proved so popular that demand far exceeded the company's data-processing capacity. Putting its core competency to work for the parent company, CompuServe took over the systems development and telecommunication functions.

Electronic filing and refund anticipation loans revolutionized the commercial tax preparation industry. The enormous demand for the product, especially among low-income taxpayers, boosted the company's share of the total tax-filing market to more than 12 percent. Suddenly the mature tax business reverted back to a growth mode.

Now in his mid-60s, Henry worked out a CEO succession plan with his son and the Block board. It called for Tom to succeed Henry as president of the company in 1989. Three years later, Tom would become CEO. Although Henry was in excellent health and had not lost an ounce of interest in the business, he was proud to begin transferring the reins to the next generation. He knew it was time. "Stockholders deserved a CEO who was younger and had a better understanding of technology," he says.

Clearly Tom would have colossal shoes to fill. His father had compiled a record of accomplishment that few in American business could match. "Henry did a superb job of leading the company," says long-time board member Morton Sosland. "I can't imagine the company being anywhere close to where it is today without Henry."

Henry was also one of the most admired and recognizable CEOs in the country. In Kansas City and elsewhere, it was not uncommon for strangers to walk up to him and ask, "Aren't you Henry Bloch?"

In an ad for *People* magazine, his picture shared the back page of the *New York Times* with Bo Derek. He was the tax king and she was the beauty queen. The headline read, "From 1040 to 10." The *Long Island*

Newsday had a presidential preference poll. Among the candidates were Mr. Whipple, Starsky, Hutch, Sgt. Pepper, and Henry Bloch. He pitched other brands on the small screen, such as Midwest Airlines and Subaru. (After receiving a number of complaints from unions about endorsing a Japanese car, he donated the proceeds from the ads to union welfare programs.)

The end of an era was looming. As Emerson once said, "Life is a succession of lessons which must be lived to be understood." During his 36 years at the helm of H&R Block, Henry learned how to start, nurture, develop, expand, and diversify one of America's top brands. And as he made plans to let go of it, Henry continued to look forward with confidence and optimism.

A Bad Dream

On September 27, 1988, Henry and Marion were in New York City with their daughter and son-in-law, Mary Jo and Bob. Marion and Mary Jo had planned a morning of shopping before meeting their husbands for lunch.

Marion, 58 years old, awoke that morning with a sharp headache. She rarely had headaches, but she wasn't about to let this one interfere with the day's plan. Mary Jo stopped at a pharmacy to get her mother some aspirin. But the medicine didn't relieve the pain. As Mary Jo flicked through a row of dresses at a store, an outfit caught her eye. While she was trying it on, her mother looked through a rack of suits. Out of the blue, Marion felt faint. Within seconds, she became unconscious, collapsing onto the floor. Suddenly she began having violent muscle contractions. Mary Jo nearly panicked when she saw her mother on the floor. She hurried to her side, feeling her mother shaking uncontrollably. A saleswoman dialed 911.

"It seemed like forever before the ambulance came," Mary Jo recalls. "I was frightened." As she tried to comfort her mother, Mary Jo asked the same saleswoman to call her father at the Great American Health Food Bar, where the two couples were to meet for lunch.

Henry and Bob raced out of the restaurant and hailed a cab in the middle of the street. Minutes later, the taxi pulled up to the store as the medics were hoisting the stretcher into the rear of the ambulance. Henry jumped in just before the driver zipped off. It was surreal; neither of them had ever ridden in an ambulance. Henry hoped it was just a dream.

Shortly after Marion regained consciousness in the hallway of the emergency room, two doctors came to the waiting room to report their findings to Henry. They explained that the abnormality was a grand mal seizure, a malfunction of electrical activity in the brain.

After analyzing the MRI, the doctors were uncertain what had triggered the seizure. Even though Marion was back to her old self within hours, they kept her at the hospital overnight for observation. Meanwhile, Henry dozed in a chair next to her bed. Armed with more questions than answers, the two couples returned to Kansas City the next day where Henry immediately sought out a doctor who could solve the mystery.

One physician said it was probably a small stroke. But when a neurologist suggested it might be a brain tumor, Henry grew even more worried.

"Who are the top two neurosurgeons in America?" he asked his doctor friend. Two of the preeminent experts were quickly identified. One practiced at the Brain Tumor Institute at the University of California-San Francisco (UCSF), and the other was at the Mayo Clinic in Rochester, Minnesota. The night before the couple left town for back-to-back appointments in California and Minnesota, Marion had another severe headache. But she managed to get on a plane the next morning. The doctor at the Mayo Clinic was convinced it was a tumor, and he wanted to operate without delay.

In the morning of October 27, 1988, one month to the day following her grand mal seizure in New York City, Marion underwent brain surgery. Her children and their spouses flew to Minnesota. And so did their rabbi, who was a close friend.

Henry's worst fear was confirmed. It was a rapidly growing tumor, a grade three astrocytoma. Although the cancer was caught relatively early, the family was devastated. Henry was heartbroken. The doctors recommended that Marion undergo an aggressive regimen of radiation followed by chemotherapy.

Later that day, Marion came to in the intensive care unit, where she was hooked up to a variety of electrical gadgets. After opening her eyes, she slowly glanced around the room and tried to get her bearings.

Marion and Henry

She fixed her eyes on each family member. Then, in a soft, calm voice came a most unanticipated question. "Where are you going for dinner tonight?" she asked. Marion had removed the focus from herself. As always, she was looking out for others.

The prognosis for this grade of tumor is so poor that almost no one survives long, Marion's doctors told the family. True to form, Henry, who had a history of ignoring miserable odds, remained resolute. So did Marion. As she regained strength, the family was astonished by her positive state of mind. She wasn't depressed; if anything, she took comfort in knowing that her husband was so single-minded about getting her the best possible medical care and beating the disease. Marion's optimism served to raise her children's low spirits.

For radiation therapy, Henry again relied on the advice of experts. He decided on UCSF, where the couple spent a long, exhausting month. Although their four children took turns visiting them in San Francisco, Marion and Henry could hardly wait to come home to Kansas City, where she began chemotherapy.

Knowing their mother would lose her stunning red hair as a side effect of the chemo, Mary Jo and Liz had a wig made from their own hair cuttings. But Marion was more comfortable wearing a scarf instead of the hairpiece.

As grueling as the months following surgery were, Marion remained in good spirits. "She was a saint," Henry says. "She never complained. She took it all in stride."

Initially, Marion had MRIs every three months to determine whether the cancer had returned. Each time, Henry and their children seemed more anxious to receive the results than she was. The cancer didn't come back. But after several years, the effects of radiation would begin to take its toll. Little by little, her quality of life would decline.

HENRY'S DEDUCTIONS

- Don't surrender. To achieve a positive outcome during an inauspicious time, be optimistic.
- Welcome competition. It keeps you on your toes.
- Use technology as a strategic weapon.

Chapter 13

Gains and Losses

I n his prime, Henry was a nine handicap. As he got older, what he lacked in skill he made up for in competitiveness. But the twice-a-week, fair-weather golfer figured he would never make headlines on the sports page.

In 1990, a friend posed an audacious question to Henry and two other prominent Jewish men in the community: "Would you be interested in applying for membership at the Kansas City Country Club?" Then came a word of warning. "There's a chance you won't get in." Henry was well aware of the risk. Since its founding almost a hundred years earlier, the ultra-exclusive club had never admitted a Jewish member.

The other two men refused the proposal. But the thought of having access to a magnificent course with pristine greens and tree-lined fairways only a minute from his home appealed to Henry. Hoping his application wouldn't stir a controversy, he put it in the mail.

Weeks later, a phone call came from the member who had sponsored Henry's candidacy. The conversation was brief. Henry had been blackballed.

Although he was irritated, Henry managed to remain calm. "I knew my application was denied simply because I was Jewish," he says. He continued playing golf with his Jewish friends at the Jewish country club more than 20 minutes away from his home, and he considered the matter closed. But it wasn't.

"All hell broke loose," Henry says.

In *Sports Illustrated*, reporter John Garrity described the improbable incident:

> I almost cheered when I read Friday morning's front-page headline in The Kansas City Star, WATSON QUITS CLUB, CITING BIAS. . . . Tom Watson, winner of eight major golf championships and 32 PGA Tour titles, had resigned from the ultra-restrictive Kansas City Country Club to protest the club's blackballing of tax-preparation tycoon Henry Bloch.
>
> Bloch, the cofounder and chairman of H&R Block, Inc., is Jewish. Watson is not Jewish, but his wife, Linda, and their two children are. Watson said his conscience forced him to resign "out of respect for my family—my wife, my children and myself."
>
> Those close to Watson say he is torn up by the decision, and little wonder. The Kansas City Country Club has been at the center of his universe since he first appeared on its fairways in short pants, learning golf at his father's side. His longtime coach, Stan Thirsk, is the club pro and a second father to Watson. For years, when other touring pros spent the winter sharpening their games in Arizona and Florida, Watson stayed home and hit practice balls into the snow from a mat in the course superintendent's shed. . . .
>
> I was ticked off, though, when I read that Bloch's candidacy, which was sponsored by Hallmark Cards chairman Donald Hall and seconded by two other major corporate chairmen, never got to the club's board for a vote. Bloch was thwarted by a five-man membership committee. This star chamber is so secret that only the club's president and secretary know its composition. Its members may not wear hoods during their deliberations, but their performance this time was sufficient to embarrass not just the club but the city as well.

That's the galling part of the Bloch affair. I suspect that many—possibly most—of the club's members hold Henry Bloch in high regard and would welcome him as a member. Undoubtedly, others are comfortable with the idea of Hispanic, Asian or black members. But until now fear has kept decent people from speaking out.

Fear of what, you ask? Why, the greatest fear of all—that they will no longer be accepted by their peers. Sounds trivial, but social acceptance is the glue that binds a city's power elite. Mavericks don't get the big contracts, the special tax abatements, the school buildings named in their honor.

By their recent actions, Bloch's sponsors and Watson have lifted that veil of fear. Already, prominent Kansas City Country Club members are publicly distancing themselves from the bigotry. Either Bloch or another Jewish candidate will be accepted soon, they say, or there will be more resignations. "It's going to change," vows one of the reformers. "I'm convinced of that."

The place to start, if an outsider may offer a suggestion, is with that secret membership committee. Flush those scrofulous characters into the open, make them accountable for their actions, and they won't be so quick to smear and denigrate. Next, do whatever it takes to get Tom Watson back in the fold. A friend of the Watson family says, "He's hurting something fierce right now."

Watson's pain may ease when he realizes that in his children's eyes, and in ours, this single act of conscience will one day count for more than all the trophies he has won with his clubs.[1]

Henry's office was besieged with phone calls from reporters, who were eager to get a quote to include in their stories. He was unwilling to say anything derogatory, but he was willing to make a brief comment.

"It's the first time I've ever made the sports page," he simply stated.

Amid intercontinental media hype and a deafening chorus of disapproval for such blatant discrimination, Henry received a phone call from the president of the club, who happened to be a close friend. "We would like to have you as a member," he said. "Are you willing to join?"

"I would be delighted," Henry replied.

He accepted the invitation, and Watson then rejoined the country club. Henry was made to feel welcome there and made many new friends. As he enjoyed the club's amenities, he remained grateful that Tom Watson chose not to tolerate discrimination. Other Jews later joined the club, including two of Henry's children.

Transitions

The hullabaloo at the Kansas City Country Club didn't sidetrack Henry for a minute. H&R Block's revenues hit the $1 billion mark in 1990. Thanks to the popularity of its electronic filing and refund anticipation loan offerings, the firm served 17 million clients in 1991, or one out of every seven taxpayers. The company acquired another large temporary help outfit called Interim Services, and Personnel Pool of America adopted the new firm's name system-wide.

But Path, the seminar company, struggled. It depended heavily on the U.S. Postal Service to deliver brochures to prospective enrollees. As postal rates increased, the unit's profitability suffered. Not-for-profit competitors soon held a distinct advantage over Path by qualifying for a lower postage rate. Henry asked Jerry Grossman to sell the business to one of them. In 1991, Path was purchased by the American Management Association. After the disposition of Path, H&R Block continued to reach new levels of profitability. The stock reached a high for a 12th straight year. A $10,000 investment in Block stock made in 1962 returned $10 million in stock price appreciation and dividends by 1991. Among the top 500 publicly held corporations, Forbes listed H&R Block 233rd in market value and 338th in net profits. In a Chief Executive magazine study that ranked CEOs according to their companies' share growth, Henry Bloch was 22nd. Warren Buffett came in 67th.

In 1992, Block implemented the final phase of the CEO succession plan. Jerry Grossman, Henry's right-hand man for two decades, retired at age 72. "He's always worked sort of behind-the-scenes, but he's responsible for much of the success of the company," Henry said. "And he's inspired a lot of people to achieve greater success by his leadership."[2]

Tom was installed as CEO and Henry remained chairman. "I have worked for this my entire life," Henry told the *New York Times*. "It is nice to build something up and then be able to pass the running of the company on to someone in the family."[3]

But Henry didn't ride off into the sunset. "People have started asking me if I am going to retire," he said. "I don't have time to retire. I'm keeping too busy and enjoying life too much. I trust I can continue to be productive. There are new horizons and new opportunities and problems out there still to be solved."

Together, Tom and Henry took on those new opportunities and problems. They bought Meca Software, a developer of personal productivity software products, including TaxCut, a tax preparation package for the do-it-yourself market, for $45 million.

They sold Interim Services for $188.5 million. Interim had performed well over its 15 years as a Block subsidiary. But, as they told shareholders, its sale would allow them to concentrate on their two largest businesses, H&R Block Tax Services and CompuServe, and on developing related businesses with more uniform operating characteristics.

In 1994, Henry appeared on *Forbes* list of the 400 richest Americans. The magazine reported that his net worth exceeded $375 million. But he didn't act as if he was rich. He continued to buy his gas on the Missouri side of the state line instead of Kansas, where it was more expensive. When he traveled, he still brought home the shampoo and soap from his hotel bathroom. And the tax man had always kept all of his credit card receipts. Each January he hunched over his adding machine, punching in every penny of sales tax he had paid so he could take the deduction on his tax return.

In 1995, the IRS rocked the commercial tax industry once again. The agency made a significant change in its electronic return processing systems and procedures, which effectively reduced the availability of refund anticipation loans to taxpayers. As Harry Buckley, then-president of the company's tax operations, said, "On October 25, 1994, we were prepared for a busy tax season and looking forward to carrying out plans for growth." Then came the surprising IRS announcement, which threw the company's plans into a tizzy. "On October 26, we had to shelve much of what had been done and achieve in only two months what normally requires eight months of preparation." For only the second time, profits for the tax business declined.

Henry never imagined that the earnings from one of the company's subsidiaries would one day surpass the core tax business. But it happened for the first time in 1995, thanks to a record three million patrons using CompuServe's online service. And the future looked brighter than ever for the online market.

More surprising to Henry was when Tom, after nearly six years as president and three years as CEO, told him he was thinking about leaving the company. The two had several heart-to-heart sessions as Tom agonized about a new direction for his life. Henry always listened thoughtfully, receptively. But when Tom told him he had decided to resign, Henry said, "I can't believe it." He urged Tom to take some time off.

"Get out of the office and take a real vacation with [your wife] Mary," Henry said. "Think about this some more." Tom and Mary went to Aspen, but when they returned, he was settled on leaving for teaching in the inner city. (He would later cofound an urban charter school for underprivileged kids.)

"No one at the company will miss Tom more than me," a teary-eyed Henry told Block associates at a farewell luncheon for his son. For the first time, a nonmember of the Bloch family would lead the company. And as disappointed as Henry was, he nonetheless supported Tom's decision. He had always encouraged his children to follow their hearts.

A three-member search committee, which included Tom, recommended Dick Brown, vice chairman at telecommunications giant Ameritech. But after less than a year as CEO, just after Henry had both of his knees replaced, Brown announced that he was returning to the telecommunications industry. But before departing for Cable & Wireless to become its CEO, he had begun separating CompuServe from H&R Block.

The rationale for detaching the two businesses was straightforward: CompuServe had grown from a small business to a big business, and the characteristics of the computer and tax units were entirely different. Stock investors were generally attracted to one business or the other, but not both. As it became increasingly difficult to value the combined company, the board decided to undo the marriage and make CompuServe an independent, publicly-traded company. In the initial offering, Block sold 20 percent of its outstanding shares in CompuServe for $519 million. It intended to sell the remaining 80 percent within the year.

But upstart America Online (AOL) had created a new paradigm in the mid-1990s, charging a flat monthly rate of $19.99 instead of hourly rates. Consumers embraced their pricing model, and the service grew rapidly. To regain market share, CompuServe fashioned a new online service called WOW! with more attractive pricing. Unfortunately, it wasn't the sensation that the name implied.

Henry asked longtime board member Frank Salizzoni, who was president and chief operating officer of USAir Group, to succeed Dick Brown. Henry liked Frank, who was personable and down-to-earth. Frank also was familiar with the business. Unfortunately, he moved out of the turbulent airline industry at a time when the computer online industry was increasingly subject to stormy weather. The Block subsidiary, whose earnings had surpassed the tax business two years earlier, swung to a significant loss in 1997.

With CompuServe in turmoil, Block scrapped its plan to sell the remaining 80 percent. In 1998, Frank orchestrated a complex stock-for-stock transaction with telecommunications giant WorldCom. It bought CompuServe for $1.2 billion and in turn sold the distressed information services division to competitor AOL. The outcome was completely unpredictable for the once market-dominating CompuServe. But considering that Block had acquired the computer company for $23 million, it still proved to be an outstanding investment.

A Transformation

Block sold its WorldCom shares before that company went bankrupt, and it used the proceeds to embark on an aggressive plan to transform the tax company into a broad-based financial services firm. The first big step was to acquire subprime mortgage operator Option One from Fleet Financial Group for $190 million. (Subprime lenders made loans to individuals with poor credit.) To fortify Block's executive team, Frank plucked Mark Ernst from American Express to become executive vice president and chief operating officer.

Frank and Mark began building a national accounting practice by acquiring firms around the country. After gaining seven regional companies, Block bought the nonattest assets of McGladrey & Pullen, LLC, the seventh largest accounting firm in the nation. The transaction represented the largest such acquisition by a public company. Henry supported both the acquisition and the strategy. He viewed public accounting, with its upscale image, as a perfect complement to the less prestigious commercial tax preparation industry.

Block wasn't yet finished with shopping around. To leverage the brand, distribution network, and relationship with millions of customers, the new executive team sought out a large discount broker. At a cost of $850 million in cash, Olde Financial Corporation represented the largest purchase in Block's history. Henry felt uneasy about the proposed acquisition. In the end, however, he didn't oppose management's recommendation. In 2000, Olde became H&R Block Financial Advisors.

"With the acquisition of Olde, we will have in place the major building blocks to achieve our vision of becoming the preferred tax and financial partner for our clients while offering an attractive product portfolio for new Block customers," Frank said. But some analysts weren't convinced, and one rating agency put Block's debt under review for a potential downgrade.[4] Before long, Henry wished he had spoken out vigorously in opposition to the Olde deal and had voted against it.

In line with the plan he had developed years earlier, Henry retired as chairman of the board that year. He was 78 years old. In his farewell letter to company associates, he offered the same call to action that he had issued regularly throughout his career: "This is my challenge to you—to continue to give our customers more than they expect . . ." He kept his office at Block's headquarters, where he worked on personal, civic and philanthropic pursuits. "Please stop by to say hello when you're in Kansas City," he told employees and franchisees.

As he presided over his final shareholders' meeting, Henry reflected on his long career. "Building a company is a lot like raising a child," he said. "You try to instill values, purpose and character. You work hard. You take some risks. You worry a lot. Along the way, you try to provide direction and guidance, and set an example. But the child grows up and comes into its own and, if you are lucky, surprises you by accomplishing great things—things you never imagined possible. That has been so true of my life with this company. . . . As long as we adhere to high standards, I believe our customers will continue to appreciate us and our company will continue to thrive."

Frank took Henry's place as chairman. Mark moved up to president and chief executive officer and, in 2002, added the title of chairman when Frank retired from the board. Henry thought it was a mistake for the board to combine the chairman and CEO roles, and he told Mark how he felt. "In the interest of good corporate governance, I believe companies should divide the roles of CEO and chairman between two people," Henry says.

Block's ambitious plan to become the financial partner of its tax clients didn't pan out. The highly anticipated leveraging of the Block brand, offices, and customer relationships never fully materialized. "Our tax office associates didn't want to sell nontax products," Henry says. "And not enough of our tax clients wanted to buy nontax products from us." The financial performance of the Financial Advisors' unit began to weaken.

During the early 2000s, Option One was the bright spot in the Block family of companies. It experienced gargantuan growth, thanks to the booming subprime lending environment in the United States. As housing prices rose, refinancing became easier. Mortgage underwriting standards declined, and some lenders made loans based only on a homeowner's equity. Some didn't require much in the way of proof of income or a down payment. Millions of Americans who could have never qualified for a loan were suddenly given an opportunity for home ownership. But what would happen if housing prices began to fall?

Mourning

The flourishing subprime mortgage market wasn't Dick Bloch's concern. He continued waging his public fight against cancer, despite having to contend with a heart problem. Fortunately, a pacemaker helped control his heart rhythms and allowed him to lead a normal life.

Dick at a National Cancer Survivors' Day rally

Dick and Annette traveled the world. They enjoyed taking summer vacations with their children and grandchildren. In the summer of 2004, the clan went to the picturesque Montage resort in Laguna Beach, where they had a splendid holiday. As they were leaving the hotel at the end of their stay, Henry and Marion along with their children and grandchildren arrived. The two families had booked the same

One of the last photos taken of H and R together

vacation spot but, due to scheduling conflicts, their visits scarcely over-lapped. H and R were at the hotel's front desk at precisely the same time. Henry checked in as Dick checked out. Days later, Henry got a phone call at the hotel. At age 78, Dick had died suddenly of heart failure. Henry was stunned. He and his family cut short their vacation and returned to Kansas City.

Dick lived with gusto. "Life is not a dress rehearsal," he used to say. Whenever asked how he was doing, Dick answered with an enthusiastic GREAT! The entrepreneur, tycoon, philanthropist, activist, and family man excelled in his pursuits. Yet, as Annette says, "He was such a humble man."

Six decades earlier, Dick was a high-school student in Kansas City and Henry was at college in Ann Arbor, Michigan. Henry sent Dick a letter congratulating him on his birthday and on being able to obtain a driver's license. He told his younger brother, "If you live right from day to day, your future will take care of itself." Dick lived right, and he left the world a better place.

Dick and Annette were impressed with the University of Kansas Hospital, where he had his pacemaker inserted three years before his death. After he passed away, Annette gave a million dollars to the hospital to establish the Richard and Annette Bloch Heart Rhythm Center. She donated another million to the hospital's new cancer center. And later she contributed $20 million to jumpstart the University of Kansas Hospital's effort to earn the National Cancer Institute's designation as a Comprehensive Cancer Center.

"H&R Block never would have become what it is today if it weren't for Dick," Henry says. "He had such a quick mind. I admired him and his adventurous spirit. And I valued our close friendship."

HENRY'S DEDUCTIONS

- Prejudice is ignorance.
- Expect the unexpected.
- If you live right from day to day, your future will take care of itself.

Chapter 14

"Block Heads"

Like an aging father keeping tabs on his grown-up children, Henry followed the developments at H&R Block from the sidelines. No longer an insider but still a fairly sizeable individual shareholder, he made keen observations and held firm opinions. His views were based on press releases, media stories, and stock analyst reports. He kept his positions to himself and his immediate family, not wanting to interfere with management or the board.

Henry also kept a routine. He exercised in the mornings in his basement and drove himself to his office, although his hours were shorter. He continued to manage his civic and philanthropic activities as well as his personal investments. The conservative, tax-conscious investor bought mainly tax-free municipal bonds. On Mondays, he had a standing lunch with a group of old friends at the Westport Flea Market, a restaurant known for its hamburgers and curly fries. The senior citizens qualified for a special 50 percent discount on their meals. In nice weather, Henry often left the office early to play golf with friends or one of his grandchildren. But even on the golf course, in the back of his mind he was often thinking about H&R Block.

Option One, the company's flourishing subprime subsidiary, was Block's star performer in the early 2000s. In the tax operations, much of the customer growth came from selling nascent tax software products aimed at do-it-yourselfers. But Block's share of the digital market paled in comparison to the industry leader, TurboTax.

Initially, the availability of tax preparation software didn't seem to harm storefront tax firms. Most of the early adopters of computerized tax programs had prepared their own returns using pencil and paper before switching over to the new technology. But the dynamics of the tax market were about to change as more consumers would become computer literate and as tax software would become more user-friendly and affordable.

The IRS got into the act by creating the Free File Alliance, allowing taxpayers with low and moderate incomes to prepare and file their federal returns online for free. The Alliance was comprised of several private-sector tax software firms, including H&R Block. Although the company missed out on potential revenue from federal returns processed through the program, it charged a fee to prepare and file state returns online.

As the online market evolved and expanded, Block stepped up its digital efforts. But still the tax firm was highly dependent on its more lucrative retail operations. Annual profit increases from Block's tax offices generally resulted more from hikes in the average charge—considerably higher than the rate of inflation in the economy—than from pulling more customers into the outlets. Henry worried that the company's pricing strategy was too aggressive. He also worried that it was unsustainable. Worse, he thought it would prove deleterious over the long run. But again, he kept his views mostly to himself.

"I hated watching the average charge climb so fast," Henry admits. He was afraid that it didn't endear customers to the company. Finally, he decided to write a letter to the board of directors to express his views on a number of issues. Henry was convinced that the tax offices no longer offered the same compelling value to low- and middle-income taxpayers, the company's bread-and-butter clientele, as it once did. Higher fees, he also believed, impaired the company's competitive position.

Most customers seemed to be tolerant of the higher fees. Consequently, as the charge for a Block-prepared return climbed above inflation year after year, the profits of the storefront business also tended to rise. But did H&R Block, the dominant firm in the industry, lower the barriers to entry? Two national competitors, Jackson Hewitt and Liberty, were expanding aggressively. Combined, these two networks grew from about 2,000 offices in North America in 1997 to around 9,000 in 2009. They were among the fastest growing franchisors in the United States.

H&R Block still managed to hold on to its position as the world's preeminent commercial tax firm. Its growing cadre of 1,500 corporate employees moved into a sparkling 18-story headquarters in downtown Kansas City. The oval-shaped, green-glass building featured a beautiful lobby with a 20-foot tall natural stone water wall.

H&R Block moved in to its new 525,000-square-foot, $138 million headquarters in 2006

Uninterested in commuting downtown on a daily basis, Henry chose not to move in to the new headquarters. He preferred the convenience of a midtown office building that was an easy, 10-minute drive from his house.

For historical purposes, a near-replica of Henry's old office was constructed on the top floor of the new H&R Block Center. It features several of his numerous civic awards prominently displayed on shelves along one wall, a beautiful photograph of Marion on another wall, and his handsome partner's desk in the middle of the room. The reproduction of Henry's office is a popular stop for tour groups visiting the headquarters. Franchisees and employees enjoy having their picture taken in it.

"Dick and I never envisioned the company ever having such an impressive headquarters," Henry says. "Frankly, I never thought we would be able to afford anything like it."

Dick would have been outraged by the building's opulence, according to his daughter, Linda Lyon.

"He was more practical," Annette says.

Blunders

In a way, maybe it was a good thing that Dick didn't see the new headquarters or the flurry of unfavorable reports about the company in newspapers across the country. But Henry couldn't avoid the adverse publicity—and he stewed over it.

He grimaced while reading articles about Block inadvertently overstating its earnings for 2003 and 2004. He shook his head over accounts of a Block computer glitch resulting in the loss of an estimated 250,000 early-season clients. The stories about Block's miscalculation of its own state income taxes for 2004 and 2005, causing the company to pay millions of dollars in back taxes, enraged him. And he fumed over the news about New York Attorney General Eliot Spitzer suing the firm, claiming that its IRA product used deceptive marketing and seeking $250 million. (This suit was later settled, along with private class action lawsuits based on similar allegations, with Block agreeing to pay up to $20.2 million, including customer refunds.)

In February of 2006, David Letterman offered late-night television viewers his Top Ten list of H&R Block's excuses. Number seven was, "H was out sick that day and R was on jury duty." Number three was, "Hard to stay focused when you've been drinking since April 16th."[1]

The jokes about H&R Block bungling its own taxes were especially hard for Henry to take. After all, his name was on the door. "If it were the XYZ Tax Service, I don't think I would have the same attachment. I had always been proud of the company." Suddenly he became embarrassed.

"It has been one black eye after another for H&R Block this tax season," the *New York Times* wrote, "and its competitors smell blood."[2] Although he had been retired for years, Henry felt like he too had been given a black eye.

An article in the *Chicago Tribune* offered this view of the state of the company and its founder:

> Where have you gone, Henry Bloch?
>
> The co-founder of the H&R Block Inc. tax preparation firm for many years helped Americans make the best of each tax season with upbeat, personal television and radio commercials that made us feel he was in our corner.
>
> The words "I'm Henry Bloch" provided the same reassuring tone that Dave Thomas gave Wendy's International or Walt Disney gave to his namesake kingdoms. Bloch was our friend in the tax business, if such a thing was possible.
>
> Bloch, 83, is still around, with the honorary title of chairman emeritus, having stepped down as chairman in 2000. He now gives his famous name and plenty of money to a variety of worthy philanthropic causes.
>
> Under discussion in 2006 is the behavior of the world's largest tax preparation firm (whose name includes "H" for Henry, "R" for late brother Richard, and their last name with "k" substituted for "h").
>
> First, there is discussion about performance. Net income fell 69 percent in the most recent quarter, including a sizable charge for a litigation settlement. In addition, technical problems with a new software distribution strategy caused problems

early this year. Some branch offices are being closed and 600 positions cut. The company also reduced its guidance for fiscal year earnings.

Second, there is a discussion about competence. The company is restating results for fiscal 2004 and 2005 due to miscalculations that underestimated its state tax liability by about $32 million. That's embarrassing for a company helping individuals file taxes accurately.

Third, there are allegations about an investment it offers. New York Atty. Gen. Eliot Spitzer filed a lawsuit accusing H&R Block of fraudulent marketing of individual retirement accounts virtually guaranteed to lose money because of a combination of hidden fees and low interest rates. The company vigorously denies this.

Analyst ratings on the stock are a mixed bag, according to Thomson Financial, consisting of one "strong buy," one "buy," four "holds," one "underperform" and one "sell." Take your pick.

So if you think you're having a tough tax season, consider Bloch and the broad-based financial company he hatched. Both could use a reassuring friend in the tax business in this worrisome year.[3]

© *Tribune Media Service, Inc.*
All Rights Reserved. Reprinted with permission.

Things didn't seem to get much better. In 2007, the bottom fell out of the subprime mortgage market. The company's Option One unit, one of the nation's largest subprime lenders, began reporting massive losses. "The slide has been steep for Option One," *BusinessWeek* reported. "For years it was the company's breadwinner, banking $2.8 billion of pretax earnings made largely during the housing boom from 2003 to 2005; at its peak, the group accounted for 60% of its parent's profits. But as the market has turned, the unit, which H&R Block now refers to as 'discontinued operations,' has soured." The report concluded: "The losses couldn't have come at a worse time for H&R Block: Its primary business, tax preparation, has struggled in recent years. The stock has cratered by almost 20%. . . . "[4]

In 2007, Block reported its first loss ever—to the tune of $433 million. The company bled another $308 million in 2008. The *Kansas City Star* summed up the buildup of bad news: "H&R Block's brand—one of the best known in corporate America—appeared to have lost its luster."[5]

The firm that once had one of the strongest balance sheets on the New York Stock Exchange now appeared to be in a rather precarious situation. Considering how important H&R Block's reputation was to Henry, he agonized over its predicament. But the long-retired founder was now in his 80s. What could he possibly do to help the company he built?

HENRY'S DEDUCTIONS

- Don't be lured into buying a business you don't fully understand.
- Hold yourself and others accountable. Don't tolerate mediocrity.
- Avoid pursuing short-term goals that thwart long-term growth.

Chapter 15

A Fork in the Road

Henry was thrilled to read that H&R Block had signed an agreement to sell Option One, its hemorrhaging subprime mortgage unit, to Cerberus, a private investment firm. Not long afterwards, he read with considerable interest that an investment fund led by Richard Breeden, a former SEC chairman turned activist investor, was waging a proxy contest. Breeden Partners wanted to replace three Block board members with a handpicked slate, which included Richard Breeden himself. It was a bitter fight.

"It is unfortunate that a dissident hedge fund, Breeden Partners, has chosen to launch a distracting proxy contest," CEO Mark Ernst wrote shareholders. "In our view, Breeden Partners has put forth no new ideas to improve shareholder value. In fact, many of Breeden Partners' proposed 'changes' are identical to actions that your company announced and began implementing before Breeden Partners acquired a single share."[1]

Richard Breeden offered a contrasting view. "As shareholders, we believe that five years is long enough to wait for H&R Block to achieve attractive returns for shareholders. This board needs fresh perspectives and new energy, which we intend to supply, to tackle the company's problems."[2]

After weighing the different arguments, Henry decided that the company could benefit from fresh perspectives and new energy. But he did not make his opinion widely known. In the end, the stockholders' vote represented a crushing defeat for Block's executive management and board.

It wasn't long before Block's CFO stepped down. Shortly thereafter, Mark Ernst resigned as chairman, president and CEO. Richard Breeden was elected chairman. (The IRS later hired Mark as deputy commissioner for operations support.) The board brought in Alan Bennett, a former CFO of health insurer Aetna, as interim CEO. Alan, who arrived in Kansas City in November of 2007, found out that Henry stopped by the corporate headquarters every week or so to cosign form letters recognizing the service anniversaries of associates. Henry wanted to meet Alan. But the interim CEO was always on the phone or in a meeting, so Henry left without disturbing him.

"Here was the man who had founded the company, who had engineered its profitability and growth, who created its internal culture and strong brand image and awareness," Alan says. "And he was too polite and thoughtful to interrupt my work."

Alan made sure the two of them met the next time Henry was at the headquarters. "From this point on we spent time each week talking," Alan says. They talked about all things Block. "Henry always spoke in a soft, humble way. He is a great listener and acutely interested in the tax business. He is also interested in the opinions of others. He listened to the complex issues I faced. Every time we met, he thanked me for helping the company resolve its issues."

"There was always a buzz around the office when he came to visit," Alan continues. "The associates of the company revere him, and he makes time for everyone."

Alan immediately confronted Block's challenges. He tightened the belt on spending and reduced the company's debt. But the pending sale of Option One fell through as conditions in the subprime market continued to deteriorate.

Billionaire Wilbur Ross, a well-known buyer of beaten-down, financially failing companies, stepped forward in March of 2008 to buy what was left of Option One. To bring Block closer to its tax roots, the weakened H&R Block Financial Advisors unit, formerly known as Olde Financial, was sold. Ameriprise Financial bought the underperforming business for $315 million in cash. Taking into account the cost and sales price for Olde, its performance as a unit of Block, and the distraction it created for the organization, Henry deemed the acquisition to have been bad for Block. But he applauded the board's decision to divest itself of Olde as well as Option One.

Hitting a Wall

Russ Smyth, a 21-year veteran of McDonald's, was hired to take on the CEO role after the 2008 filing season. It seemed like a perfect fit. H&R Block was often called the McDonald's of the tax business. Russ says the two companies shared a common "brand DNA." Both had a strong family heritage, and both were pioneers in franchising. "They appeal to middle America—all age groups, income demographics, races, creeds, and colors. And both companies grew to be successful on a simple philosophy: If you provide customers with products and services at a fair price, you'll have people lined out the door."

Amid one of the most severe economic recessions in the nation's history, fewer people were in line outside Block's door during Russ's first tax season at the helm. Many retailers aggressively cut prices in early 2009 as the economy contracted and unemployment escalated. It was Henry's strong opinion that Block's tax outlets should have followed suit, with the support of a strong advertising campaign promoting lower prices. But when the season ended, the average fee in the offices had again increased more than the rate of inflation, and the number of taxpayers using the company's storefronts had decreased by nearly one million. Yet profits managed to rise, thanks to broad cost reductions and higher fees.

Russ knew Block had, as he says, "hit a wall." For him, it was déjà vu; McDonald's had faced a similar situation several years earlier. "People were saying that McDonald's was going the way of old iconic brands that had lost their way," according to Russ. "They were losing market share and relying too much on price to drive revenue and profitability." McDonald's responded by making changes.

Block made some changes, too. There were personnel moves. The operation became leaner. Russ retained a marketing consultant who helped engineer the turnaround at McDonald's. And he communicated to the organization that the main focus in the future would be on increasing market share. "We must start with the customers, not the P&L," he says.

Russ reached out to Henry, who was delighted to be consulted. Over one of their lunches, Henry asked Russ about his business philosophy. Russ told him that he was determined to create a more client-centric culture, and he vowed to halt the reliance on hefty fee increases.

Russ asked Henry about the golden years of the company, the secret sauce, the magic formula. He was struck by Henry's humility. "Henry immediately gives credit to others for things that went well and always takes the blame for things that didn't work out," Russ says. "I think that's the sign of a strong leader. There's something about him that resonates integrity and character."

At the annual meeting of shareholders following Russ's first tax season, he offered a frank assessment. "We don't do a good job of taking care of our clients," he said. "That's why our retention rate [of clients] was 68 percent this last tax season and has typically been between 68 and 70 percent historically."[3] Henry was pleased to hear the CEO deliver such a candid appraisal to shareholders. He hoped his forthrightness would translate into a sensible and responsive growth plan for the 2010 tax season that would then be successfully executed.

The plan didn't include across-the-board price cuts backed by an aggressive marketing program to highlight the reduced fees. "Price is part of the puzzle, but it's not the whole puzzle," Russ says. "Customers are looking for value. Our fee increases exceeded the rate of inflation for more than a decade. When a company does that, it better make sure that service quality improves. What we are faced with is fixing the value equation."

Russ mapped out a broad vision. "We have barely scratched the surface as far as what technology can do for our business," he says. "The line is blurring between getting your taxes done in a retail outlet and doing it at home. People are looking for hybrid solutions that don't fit neatly between the retail and digital buckets. People are looking for choices based on their needs."

Meanwhile, the IRS mapped out a plan to regulate the U.S. tax preparation industry. Professional preparers would have to be registered, they would be required to take and pass a competency test, and they would be obligated to meet continuing education requirements.

"Tax return preparers help Americans with one of their biggest financial transactions each year," says IRS commissioner Doug Shulman. "We must ensure that all preparers are ethical, provide good service, and are qualified. At the end of the day, tax preparers and the associated industry must be part of our overall game plan to strengthen the integrity of the tax system."[4] Regulating the tax preparation industry was what Henry had advocated since the early 1970s.

"It will clean up a part of the industry that doesn't have high standards," Russ says. "Block's standards will exceed the IRS requirements." But the new regulatory requirements would not affect the 2010 filing season.

Russ expected better results in 2010, even without new industry regulations. "We believe there are three keys to our success; operational excellence, leadership marketing and strong financial discipline," he told investors on an earnings call. "In terms of operational excellence, we are working to attract and retain more clients by improving the quality and consistency of the client experience and delivering greater value to all of our clients regardless of whether they visit our offices, use our online software, or choose some combination of both."[5]

While management was looking ahead to the next tax season, Henry couldn't shake his displeasure with the firm's performance in the last one. It was now two years since a dissident slate of directors had been elected, and Henry was growing impatient. The need for a bold plan to regain market share was, he believed, more urgent than ever.

When the company issued earnings guidance to the investment community that reflected a positive outlook for 2010, Henry surmised two things. First, there was no basis for optimism without a convincing, game-changing tax season plan. Second, it was a mistake to issue earnings guidance.

More Taxing Times

The 2010 tax season began in a downbeat way for Block. The company announced in mid-season that it had lost customers and had also lost ground to competitors. And once again, the average fee increased in the tax offices, albeit by the smallest amount in many years. Block withdrew its earnings guidance.

In a mid-season article in *Barrons.com* entitled "Take Your Chips off H&R Block," the reporter stated: "[Management] was promising changes to draw new customers to its stores and its fledgling digital presence. Instead, the last few weeks have been disastrous for H&R Block (ticker:HRB). The nation's largest tax preparer is losing customers at a fast clip, leading to questions about whether the company is mired in a perpetual decline." The reporter quoted an equity analyst, who summed up the company's performance this way: "They're losing the battle on all fronts."[6]

"It's not immediately clear to us that the premium cost of H&R Block's retail tax services can be reasonably justified given TurboTax's very user-friendly, lower-cost offerings," another analyst stated. "We suspect that many consumers are concluding that H&R Block's value proposition is simply not compelling."[7]

The Block board had authorized a $2 billion stock repurchase program targeted between 2009 and 2012. Henry felt that before repurchasing shares, the company should first demonstrate that the core business could achieve sustainable revenue and earnings growth by increasing its market share. But the buyback began before the firm proved that its competitive edge had been permanently restored.

Henry was perplexed by other decisions. For instance, at the new Yankee Stadium, there was the H&R Block Suite Level and the H&R Block Suite Lounge Board Room. There was also an H&R Block billboard. Henry knew that tax season and baseball season scarcely overlap. He was also sure that Block clients don't typically purchase seats in expensive stadium suites.

On Opening Day of the sparkling new stadium, the gigantic HD scoreboard showed the H&R Block Tax Tip of the Day. That day happened to be April 16th, the day *after* tax season had ended. One reporter said it "seemed ill-timed."[8] And in another article, entitled

"H&R Block Sponsorship at Yankee Stadium Needs an Audit," the author wrote, "The tax preparation company's pact with the New York Yankees, which calls for their green block logo to be adorned around Yankee Stadium, stands out as one of the biggest sports sponsorship head-scratchers in recent years."[9]

Looking back at the proxy contest in 2007, Breeden Capital Management told investors that one of the key issues facing the Block board was the company's "future strategy for growth."[10] Henry was of the same mind. But three tax seasons later, Henry still felt this was an acute issue for the company's core business.

Back in 2008, CEO Russ Smyth spoke with investors about leading H&R Block "back to being a great company again." He said, "We'll grow our client base by improving client satisfaction and retention for existing customers."[11] Those words were music to Henry's ears. But over the next two tax seasons, as the nation's unemployment rate swelled to 10 percent, the client base contracted by a staggering amount—a loss that was approaching two million customers.

Henry knew that H&R Block was experiencing one of the most taxing times in its 55-year history. Yet he remained confident that the board and management could mastermind a turnaround. So did a stock analyst, who made his point by repeating the tag line from the firm's TV commercials: "We think that over the next couple of years HRB has the brand, the financial products, and the opportunity to finally 'get it right.'"[12]

But what was the right strategy for the core retail business? Did it involve promoting lower prices? Or did it call for raising prices or keeping them flat? As the 2011 tax season loomed, two things were clear to Henry. First, the company was at a terribly important fork in the road. And second, it was not too late for H&R Block to become a great and a growing company again.

But it became evident in the summer of 2010 that Russ Smyth would not be the one to lead Block back to greatness. Less than two years into his tenure, he resigned. Henry wasn't surprised. For a number of reasons the last two tax seasons had been disappointing and difficult, to say the least.

Board member and former Interim CEO Alan Bennett returned to the helm. Henry figured Alan would at least have a better grasp of the magnitude of the task at hand than someone from outside the company who was unfamiliar with the challenges. Yet Henry knew that righting the ship for long-term success would not be easy for anyone.

Instead of falling into despair, Henry had renewed hope that the new CEO understood the need to aggressively promote lower prices to regain market share, reinvigorate the brand, and achieve sustainable growth. With Ralph Waldo Emerson, Henry agrees: "When it is dark enough, you can see the stars."

HENRY'S DEDUCTIONS

- Don't underestimate the power of low prices.
- In business, you're measured not by your intentions but by your results.
- Everybody makes mistakes, but not everybody learns from them.

Chapter 16

A Taxing System

For decades, Henry Bloch was America's tax man. He was the face of the company that had an uncommonly close personal relationship with more taxpayers than anyone. They trusted him. They believed he understood their concerns. And he felt a genuine responsibility to stand up for them whenever Congress debated amending the tax code.

But it wasn't a role that Henry came to naturally. When he first started out in business, he wasn't all that comfortable and skilled as a public speaker. And when first called upon to testify on tax reform before a Congressional committee, he got nervous. With experience, however, he became an increasingly relaxed and convincing speaker. And he grew to become one of the nation's foremost advocates for average, middle-income taxpayers, the same people who use H&R Block's services. Arguably, no one had a better grasp of their interests. Yet their voice, he knew, was too often ignored in tax deliberations in Washington, D.C.

Over the years, Henry has heard a plethora of anecdotes, yarns, grumbles, and barks about the tax code. But as a student of tax history and the U.S. tax system for more than a half-century, he has concluded that in at least one respect, our income tax system is a model for the world.

"A self-assessment system works only if taxpayers are honest," he says. "Unlike taxpayers in some countries, the vast majority of Americans make every effort to comply with their government's tax laws." Of course there will always be a few who try to beat the system.

Will Rogers said, "The income tax has made more liars out of the American people than golf." Nonetheless, most taxpayers dread the thought of receiving a letter from the IRS. This fear, according to Henry, is not necessarily a bad thing.

"An effective and tough enforcement agency keeps people honest," he says. Every April, newspapers offer tips on how to avoid an audit— and so do comedians.

"Worried about an IRS audit?" Jay Leno asked. "Avoid what's called a red flag. That's something the IRS always looks for. For example, say you have some money left in your bank account after paying taxes. That's a red flag."

Henry tells the joke about an anxious taxpayer who was meeting with an IRS agent during an audit. "We at the IRS consider it a great privilege to live and work in the United States," the auditor said. "All citizens have a responsibility to pay their fair share of taxes, and I expect you to pay yours with a smile."

"Thank goodness," the taxpayer responded. "I thought you were going to want cash."

Like a numismatic enjoys rare coins, Henry enjoys clever one-liners about taxes. The most famous is attributed to Benjamin Franklin, who said, "In this world nothing can be said to be certain, except death and taxes."

"At least there's one advantage about death," Henry quotes former solicitor general Erwin Griswold. "It doesn't get worse every time Congress meets."

Tax History

Henry has examined the evolution of taxes throughout the civilized world. The first known tax was instituted more than 4,000 years ago in ancient Egypt. Since then, practically every country has imposed a variety of taxes on their citizens, some of them rather dubious. Four hundred years ago, for example, Ireland introduced a window tax. The amount paid by a homeowner was based on the number of windows in his house. Three hundred years ago, Russia placed a tax on men who sported beards. Apparently Peter the Great felt strongly that men should be clean-shaven. Not long ago some states introduced a tax for possessing illegal drugs. After acquiring a banned substance, a buyer must report and pay the tax.

Taxes in America predated the Declaration of Independence. When colonists were required to pay hefty duties on imports, they protested the taxes imposed on them by the British Parliament. Taxation without representation led to the Boston Tea Party and eventually the Revolutionary War. But as humorist Gerald Barzan discovered, "Taxation with representation ain't so hot either."

The first U.S. income tax began in 1862. That's also when the Internal Revenue Service was created. The tax form comprised only 10 lines. The purpose of the tax, signed into law by President Lincoln, was to fund the Civil War. It was repealed 10 years later.

Many developed countries already had an income tax when President Cleveland proposed and Congress approved reinstituting it in 1894. But a 2 percent tax on incomes over $4,000 proved too much for many Americans to swallow. The Supreme Court declared it unconstitutional.

By 1913, enough states ratified the 16th Amendment to the Constitution: "The Congress shall have power to lay and collect taxes on incomes, from whatever source derived, without apportionment among the several States, and without regard to any census or enumeration," the amendment states.

Whenever Henry gave tax talks, he handed out copies of the first Form 1040, also introduced in 1913. It was three pages long. The top rate was 7 percent—a 1 percent tax plus a 6 percent surtax. But the relatively low rates and simple form were short-lived; Congress began tinkering with the income tax as economic and social conditions changed.

Rates soared to 77 percent in 1918 to pay for World War I. During World War II, incomes above $200,000 were taxed at a whopping 94 percent.

TO BE FILLED IN BY COLLECTOR.   Form 1040.   TO BE FILLED IN BY INTERNAL REVENUE BUREAU.

List No. ....   **INCOME TAX.**   *File No.* ....

.... *District of* ....   **THE PENALTY**   *Assessment List* ....
                                          FOR FAILURE TO HAVE THIS RETURN IN
Date received ....   THE HANDS OF THE COLLECTOR OF   *Page* .... *Line* ....
                                          INTERNAL REVENUE ON OR BEFORE
                                          MARCH 1 IS $20 TO $1,000.
                                          (SEE INSTRUCTIONS ON PAGE 4.)

UNITED STATES INTERNAL REVENUE.

RETURN OF ANNUAL NET INCOME OF INDIVIDUALS.
(As provided by Act of Congress, approved October 3, 1913.)

RETURN OF NET INCOME RECEIVED OR ACCRUED DURING THE YEAR ENDED DECEMBER 31, 191....
(FOR THE YEAR 1913, FROM MARCH 1, TO DECEMBER 31.)

Filed by (or for) .... *of* ....
                        (Full name of individual.)   (Street and No.)

In the City, Town, or Post Office of .... *State of* ....
                        (Fill in page 2 and 3 before making entries below.)

1. Gross Income (see page 2, line 12)	$			
2. General Deductions (see page 3, line 7)	$			
3. Net Income	$			

Deductions and exemptions allowed in computing income subject to the normal tax of 1 per cent.

4. Dividends and net earnings received or accrued, of corporations, etc., subject to like tax. (See page 2, line 11)........	$		
5. Amount of income on which the normal tax has been deducted and withheld at the source. (See page 2, line 9, column A)..			
6. Specific exemption of $3,000 or $4,000, as the case may be. (See Instructions 3 and 19)			

Total deductions and exemptions. (Items 4, 5, and 6) .... | $ |

7. Taxable Income on which the normal tax of 1 per cent is to be calculated. (See Instruction 3). | $ |

8. When the net income shown above on line 3 exceeds $20,000, the additional tax thereon must be calculated as per schedule below:

			INCOME.	TAX.
1 per cent on amount over $20,000 and not exceeding $50,000....	$		$	
2 " " " 50,000 " " 75,000....				
3 " " " 75,000 " " 100,000....				
4 " " " 100,000 " " 250,000....				
5 " " " 250,000 " " 500,000....				
6 " " " 500,000				

Total additional or super tax .... | $ |

Total normal tax (1 per cent of amount entered on line 7).... | $ |

Total tax liability........................... | $ |

The first Form 1040 was introduced in 1913

According to Henry, one of the more significant tax laws in our nation's history was the Revenue Act of 1943. It introduced a pay-as-you-go requirement. Taxpayers were obligated to stay current on their tax by paying throughout the year. And employers were responsible for withholding taxes from their employees' paychecks.

As the income tax system continually changed and grew more complex, tax reform became an increasingly contentious topic among lawmakers and voters. Henry recognized the dilemma that elected representatives faced as they considered revising tax laws and rates. The crux of the problem for lawmakers was whether they should do what was right or merely what their constituents wanted. Cutting taxes, for example, is fashionable, but it might not be fiscally responsible. Simplifying taxes is also politically popular, but it might create inequities.

Tax Policy

Political rants about tax reform are never louder than during peak election cycles. Both Republican and Democratic presidential candidates have been known to make vigorous if not audacious statements about our tax system.

Jimmy Carter blasted the federal income tax system, labeling it "a disgrace to the human race."[1]

Calvin Coolidge exclaimed, "Collecting more taxes than necessary is legalized robbery."

George H. W. Bush pledged: "Read my lips: no new taxes." This line may have helped him get elected. But after taxes were raised during his first term, he lost his reelection bid.

Presidential candidate Steve Forbes didn't mince words when assessing the tax system: "We can't tinker with this tax code monstrosity or try to reform it around the edges. The only thing we can do with this hideous beast is kill it, drive a stake through its heart, bury it, and hope it never rises again to terrorize the American people!"

Before being elected governor of California, Ronald Reagan quoted Harvard economist Sumner Slichter. He was the Harvard professor whose writings inspired Henry to start his own business. Quoting Slichter, Reagan said, "If a visitor from Mars looked at our tax policy, he would conclude it had been designed by a Communist spy to make free enterprise unworkable." Reagan went on to say: "But we cannot have such reform while our tax policy is engineered by people who view the tax as a means of achieving changes in our social structure."[2]

In a speech Henry gave in Chicago in 1976, he rebuffed the kind of politically popular views that Slichter, Reagan, and others had ballyhooed. Here is an excerpt:

> Our system of taxes was born to provide solely for the dollars necessary to pay the costs of running the government. Today,

however, the scope of taxation has broadened to include financial solutions to various social and economic problems and rightly so.

Just as we have adjusted to living in a society far removed from simpler times in our nation's history, we must adjust to the fact that there's nothing simple about taxes and never will be. Simplification can be a goal, but we must always keep a balance between simplification and equity. Behind the seductive rhetoric of one simple tax structure for all are pitfalls that would literally destroy the basic principle of everyone paying their fair share.

Tax laws and tax forms cannot be reduced to child's play without destroying the integrity of a system intended to make everyone pay a fair share based on means and to encourage desirable social and economic goals, whether they be charitable contributions or more construction jobs and home ownership.

President Reagan signed into law one of the nation's most sweeping pieces of tax legislation, the Tax Reform Act of 1986. Among other changes, it reduced the top tax rates, broadened the tax base, increased the home mortgage deduction, eliminated tax shelters, and expanded the alternative minimum tax. Reagan equated the legislation to the game of baseball: "I feel that we just played the World Series of Tax Reform, and the American taxpayer won."

Like most tax legislation, there were some essential provisions in the 1986 act. But, as is the norm, there were losers as well as winners. As Henry told a group of Block associates, "some [taxpayers] will view it either as a curve ball, others as a fast ball, a pitchout, or even a screwball." At another Block meeting, he said, "I see a whole new era of tinkering that will last for a decade." He was right on both counts.

Some politicians have proposed throwing out our income tax system and replacing it with a national sales tax. However, as Henry is quick to point out, a sales tax is regressive; the people who would pay the highest share of their total income in taxes are the economically disadvantaged. "A consumption tax shifts the burden from the rich to the poor," he says.

In H&R Block's 1985 annual report, Henry addressed various federal tax changes that were under consideration at the time. The same kinds of proposals are debated today in our nation's capital. Henry wrote:

> Should a taxpayer with an income of $1 million or more pay the same rate as one with $200,000, $100,000, or $75,000? Are the additional brackets needed to achieve fairness really that complex? For all its flaws, the current tax code seeks to collect more from the rich than from the poor, and the additional brackets add an element of fairness which three brackets . . . could never achieve.
>
> Existing credits, deductions, and exemptions were deemed to be worthwhile when they were enacted. Yet many of these deductions and credits would be curtailed, eliminated, or lose their effectiveness under reform proposals.
>
> If reform is enacted, over time the tax laws will almost certainly be amended to add back most of the same deductions and credits that had been removed because the legitimate social, economic, and political needs would still exist and remain otherwise unmet.
>
> And then there's the rule of unintended consequences:
> * Would charitable contributions be given less freely if the deduction were worth less because of reduced tax rates?
> * What effect would the proposals have on employment in the housing industry?
> * What would be the impact on the states that base their taxes on federal rules as to what constitutes taxable income?
>
> These questions cannot be ignored; the more radical the change in the tax laws, the more significant will be the unintended consequences.
>
> We should carefully examine the tax code and eliminate or simplify provisions where the complexity is not worth the problems it causes. Abusive tax shelters should be eliminated, and taxpayers should pay a minimum amount of tax in relation to their income.
>
> A certain amount of complexity is the price we pay for fairness and the achievement of economic and social goals.

Thoughtless simplification could be very destructive to our economic and social system.

Henry once heard Jack Kemp, the former Buffalo Bills quarterback turned politician, speak at a hotel ballroom in Kansas City. Kemp had run unsuccessfully for the Republican presidential nomination and was later a vice presidential running mate. Henry, who in recent years has cast his vote for as many Democratic candidates as Republicans, had a brief conversation with Kemp at a small private reception before his address. "He couldn't have been nicer," Henry recalls. "A very personable guy."

The politically conservative audience listened intently and applauded frequently as the charismatic Kemp delivered his speech to the filled room. At one point, he talked about tax reform. An outspoken Flat Tax advocate, he wanted to make taxes "flatter, fairer, simpler, and lower." He also wanted to "get rid of the IRS's intrusiveness into our pockets, our lives and into our property."

Kemp suddenly veered away from his standard talking points: "*I want to put Henry Bloch out of business!*" Henry was taken aback. But he didn't take the former Congressman's remark personally. He knew that tax simplification made excellent political fodder.

Lord Bramwell observed, "Like mothers, taxes are often misunderstood, but seldom forgotten." In the case of the Flat Tax, taxpayers are initially attracted to the notion of a 1040 the size of a postcard and a single, lower tax rate. But many of them simply don't understand its implications.

"As soon as you tell taxpayers they'll have to surrender their tax deductions and credits," Henry says, "they tend to turn against the plan." He also emphasizes that it is the rich who would benefit from a Flat Tax. Henry is a strong proponent of a progressive tax system whereby top-income earners pay a higher rate of tax than bottom-income earners. "Because the wealthy have more disposable income than the poor, they have an ability to pay tax at a higher rate."

No matter the type of the tax, the length of the form, or the rate, there will always be critics. Someone said that the people who complain about taxes can be divided in two groups—men and women. Or, as Henry says, quoting Senator Russell Long: "Don't tax you. Don't tax me. Tax the fellow behind the tree."

The Ideal Tax System

What is the ideal tax system? Years ago, Henry tried to answer this question. His analysis is as applicable today as it was when he wrote the following:

> A tax system created in an atmosphere of economic compromise will always be less than perfect because it will always be changing. While some call for tax simplification, we should not confuse simplicity with fairness. Complexity is required for a system to be fair because a fair and equitable system will be sensitive to the fact that not everyone's financial situation is the same. To create a new tax system just for the sake of eliminating complexity would result in a system less equitable, less fair. I feel strongly that such a change would be a serious mistake.
>
> I believe in a tax system that is fair. In my mind, tax fairness is based primarily on a person's ability to pay, which requires both graduated tax rates and a broad tax base. Any reform should preserve the fairness of a comprehensive and moderately progressive tax system.
>
> I also believe in a tax system that is simple. However, our tax system not only generates revenue, it also is used by our government to achieve economic and social objectives. In our complex society, objectives frequently change. Our tax system has been used to provide incentives that promote public goals. For example, by allowing deductions and credits, the tax system promotes economic expansion. The deduction for charitable contributions motivates taxpayers to give to worthwhile organizations whose existence is dependent upon such donations. By allowing taxpayers to deduct their home mortgage interest and taxes, the tax system makes it easier for individuals to achieve their personal goal of home ownership. By providing a refundable earned income tax credit, the tax system encourages and rewards people who work their way out of poverty.
>
> As long as we have a democratic society, our nation's priorities and policies will change. Whether the issue is tackling the budget deficit or maintaining our competitiveness in

the international market place, we Americans are faced with a number of national challenges. To meet these challenges and attain our goals, tax laws must often be modified, thus creating what is viewed as additional complexity.

The dynamic tension between fair and flexible is what makes the American tax system the envy of the world. As we work to improve our tax system, we should not sacrifice what works well. Responsible change that promotes good public policy and tax fairness is to be welcomed.

Practically every tax season, editorial cartoons that mention H&R Block in some context appear in newspapers across the country. One of them shows a 911 operator telling a caller, "We're only allowed to connect you to the police, fire department, or hospital . . . you'll have to call H&R Block yourself."

Another shows an unshaven, scowling pair of entrepreneurs, Henry and Richard, manning a hot-dog cart on a downtown sidewalk. As a well-dressed couple walk up to the brothers to buy a hot dog, the

"WHATEVER YOU DO, DON'T ASK THEM ABOUT THE DAYS BEFORE TAX REFORM."

One of the many editorial cartoons mentioning H&R Block that have appeared in newspapers over the years

husband turns to his wife, saying, "Whatever you do, don't ask them about the days before tax reform."

And one more has an H&R Block tax office attached to the White House, with President Obama telling Uncle Sam, "We decided it would come in handier than a vegetable garden."

"WE DECIDED IT WOULD COME IN HANDIER THAN A VEGETABLE GARDEN."

Another editorial cartoon that refers to H&R Block

The fictional cartoon character Alfred E. Neuman said, "Today it takes more brains and effort to make out the income tax form than it does to make the income." As long as there is a constantly changing, complex tax system, it's a safe bet that many, if not most, people will turn to a professional preparer or a digital tax preparation product. About 80 percent of U.S. taxpayers currently use professionals, desktop tax software, or online tax sites.

Henry doesn't suggest that all taxpayers are better off making use of a professional preparer. "To be honest, people would be better off doing their own returns *if* they know taxes," he says. "It would help them with their financial planning. But most people don't know taxes well enough to do their own returns. Many do-it-yourselfers tend to overpay by missing out on deductions and credits."

When Henry once testified before the House Ways and Means Committee, a fellow panelist, who was a distinguished university professor, told the committee that the government should be very appreciative of firms like H&R Block. If they didn't exist, the professor went on to say, imagine the condition of millions of tax returns that would arrive at the IRS every year.

Regardless of how one feels about taxes, there is a light side to the annual burden of complying with the federal tax code. Henry has heard more amusing tax stories about his firm's clients than he can remember.

In one Block outlet, a client learned that his young son was worth $3,500 as an exemption on his tax return. So the man conveyed the good news to his son. The boy turned to his father. "If I'm worth that much on your taxes," the boy said, "don't you think I should get more than a dollar-a-week allowance?"

Another client was adamant about claiming her dog as a dependent. "He's more loyal than my children!" she insisted.

One Block office prepared a joint return for a jailed bank robber and his wife. The husband had insisted that his wife go to H&R Block to have their return prepared because he didn't want to also be charged with tax evasion.

Entrepreneur magazine wrote, "If Henry Bloch has a lucky day, it's got to be April 15—a day most Americans dread. While the rest of us moan, groan, and grumble at the thought of filing our income tax returns, Bloch beams and grins at the thought of the millions of people who are turning to his company for help."[3]

The *Wall Street Journal* once described the weeks between January 1st and April 15th as "the season of the year when we discover that we owe most of our success to Uncle Sam." But that's not the case for Henry. He owes *all* of his success to Uncle Sam—and to the ordinary, honest taxpayers behind the 500 million returns that his firm has prepared.

HENRY'S DEDUCTIONS

- Be a political advocate for your customers.
- Promote public policy that is good, not merely self-serving.
- True leaders understand that trying to please everybody doesn't work.

Chapter 17

Opening Doors

H enry Wash was abandoned at birth. When his classroom teacher told him he would never be able to learn, he broke down in tears and ran home.

"Never let anyone tell you what you can't do," his foster mother said.

Each afternoon after school, Wash worked as a sacker at a grocery store. In 2000, he enrolled at Kansas City's Penn Valley Community College and took a job as a fitness attendant at an athletic club. But he didn't make enough to stay in junior college. Shortly after dropping out, he received a phone call from an academic coach at the school, notifying him of a new scholarship opportunity, called the Henry W. Bloch Scholars program. Wash submitted his application, hoping for the best.

The H&R Block Foundation established the program in 2000 in honor of Henry's retirement from the company. It awards 90 scholarships annually to Kansas City students who would otherwise not be considered for a traditional scholarship due to academic performance or other life circumstances. Scholars receive tuition and fees at one of two local community colleges. After earning an associates degree, they can continue on at the University of Missouri–Kansas City (UMKC) for a bachelor's degree. Scholarships are automatically renewed as long as students meet certain requirements, including maintaining a 2.5 grade-point average.

"The Scholars program is the best gift I have ever received," Henry Bloch says. "I was an average student and had to work very hard to make passing grades. Many of the Scholars remind me of myself when I was their age."

"The Bloch Scholars program typifies Henry," Ed Matheny, a member of the foundation board and a close friend of Henry's, says.

The Bloch Scholars meet with academic coaches at their colleges. The coaches connect the students to resources—tutors, transportation, childcare, etc. They also provide encouragement when the students need motivation. The foundation feels so strongly about the value of academic coaches that it funds this component at the community colleges and at UMKC. The foundation also established an emergency assistance fund to help students handle urgent financial problems that may arise, such as car repairs and rent payments.

Each semester, Henry visits with the Scholars, has lunch with them, and generally makes himself available as a mentor. He always asks new Scholars if they are the first in their families to attend college. In most cases, they are.

As a recipient of the scholarship, Henry Wash was thrilled to return to Penn Valley Community College. When he met Henry Bloch there, Wash discovered they had more in common besides the same first name and middle initial.

"I told Mr. Bloch that I'm not smart but I work hard. He told me he was the same way." Wash later graduated from UMKC, majoring in sociology and minoring in African American studies.

"I wanted to honor Henry Bloch by getting a graduate degree in urban affairs from the Henry W. Bloch School of Business and Public Administration," Wash says. And he did just that.

The Bloch School

Ed Smith, a former board member of both H&R Block and the H&R Block Foundation, had the idea of renaming UMKC's business school after Henry Bloch. Henry was unaware of Ed's plan until the arrangements were nearly finalized in 1986. "I was deeply honored," Henry says.

The Bloch School followed a traditional business curriculum until 2005, when it began emphasizing the development of entrepreneurial and innovative leaders. That year it established the Institute for Entrepreneurship and Innovation (IEI), with the lofty vision of creating the world's leading research and education program of its kind.

The Henry W. Bloch School of Business and Public Administration at the University of Missouri-Kansas City

Henry is excited about the school's focus, and he is helping it reach its goal. He established the school's endowment board and still serves as its chairman. He has donated millions of dollars endowing scholarships and professorships. And he has contributed countless hours in the classroom.

"I would like to see the Bloch School ranked as one of the best schools in the country," Henry says. So would Dr. Teng-Kee Tan, the school's dean.

Teng-Kee is one of the first Chinese-American deans of a U.S business school. He has lived and worked in six countries and on three continents. And he has broad academic and business experience, including 18 years in the corporate world, nine of them as an entrepreneur. Before coming to the Bloch School, he founded and led one of the world's premier entrepreneurship programs, located in Singapore. In large part, he was attracted to Kansas City because of Henry's aspirations for the school and the community's high expectations for its urban university.

An editorial about the dean states, "His audacious goals include turning the Bloch School into one of the nation's top programs, partly by doubling enrollment and tripling the faculty count in the next five years."[1]

An out-of-the-box thinker, Teng-Kee has begun creating what he calls "the American business school of the twenty-first century." He explains that, "as the country reinvents its values and economy, universities must reinvent the way we educate the next generation. Experiential learning, global immersion, and entrepreneurial leadership are key."[2] The bottom line, he says, is to make business school students "market ready." That requires real-world experience *before* they graduate. "The new pedagogy is a synthesis of structure and chaos, learning by doing on the fly. We are putting their feet to the fire."

In 2009, the IEI was recognized by the Princeton Review as one of the Top 25 graduate entrepreneurship programs in the country. "The importance of this accomplishment is more than just the ranking," Henry says. "The Bloch School and UMKC are creating the next generation of entrepreneurs."

By merging theory with practical application, the business school forms relationships with other disciplines across the university. Students in the law school, the medical school, and even the music school are learning about entrepreneurship and innovation. The business school is also reaching out to the local business and civic community. As its web site states, "More than 13,000 Bloch alumni live and work in the greater Kansas City area, forming a powerful network."

But much work lies ahead before Henry and Teng-Kee's dreams are realized. "Change is never easy," the dean says, "especially when it involves tearing down the ivory tower mindset."

The Bloch Scholars

Henry Wash is one of the Bloch School's alums. He works at the United Services Community Action Agency, a nonprofit organization that helps low-income individuals achieve self-sufficiency. As a life coach at a high school, he teaches personal development and work readiness to economically disadvantaged students. "I talk to them about choices, relationships, and behaviors," he says. At the end of the program, the young people are in a position to gain and retain employment as well as to function as productive members of society.

While at the Bloch School, Wash started a mentoring program called High Aspirations. It works with young African American men in the inner city, providing social, emotional, academic, and spiritual support.

"The kids in the program are often headed for trouble," he says. "This intervention gets them headed in the right direction." Mentees engage in a variety of activities, ranging from chess to leadership development to community service.

Henry Bloch attended Henry Wash's graduations and also his wedding. And the two Henrys have lunch three or four times a year.

"He gives me good advice," Wash says. "He told me to be faithful to my wife and go out of my way to care for her. My goal is to be like him—I want to give back and help people."

Wash credits Henry Bloch and the Bloch Scholars program for changing the trajectory of his life. "I definitely wouldn't be where I am if it wasn't for Henry Bloch. People like him have a special place in heaven."

Dustin Jensen is another Bloch Scholar. When he was 25, he enrolled in evening classes at Maple Woods Community College to earn a certificate in heating and cooling. He remembers Henry Bloch telling his cohort class about being an average student. "This is something that I always felt about myself," Dustin says. "I knew that many doors are closed to people who do not excel in school. Mr. Bloch encouraged us to find our passion and work toward it."

"If it weren't for the scholarship, I would probably be doing heating and cooling somewhere," Dustin says. Instead, he is finishing up his bachelor's degree at UMKC while working at the Metropolitan Energy Center, where he is now the associate executive director. The nonprofit organization conducts energy audits and makes homes more energy efficient.

Like Henry Wash, Dustin is also giving back. He received the Vice Chancellor's Award for helping make UMKC's new student union a "green" building. And he works at a community college assisting dislocated workers to become weatherization technicians.

"I love what I'm doing," he says. "The Bloch Scholars program kept the door open for me. The H&R Block Foundation and Henry Bloch have played an important role in my life."

Fantashia Freeman worked three jobs to pay her community college expenses. "My parents weren't in a position to help," she says. An academic coach encouraged her to apply for the Bloch scholarship.

"It was amazing," she says. "The scholarship took care of the burden of juggling work and school." In 2003, she graduated from UMKC with a bachelor of arts in sociology and a double minor in cultural anthropology and Black studies.

Thanks to the financial support of the foundation, Fantashia had an opportunity to accompany her anthropology professor on a field study to Gambia and Senegal, where she worked with children infected with HIV/AIDS. "That trip changed my life," she says. On a follow-up trip, she volunteered at a hospice for children with the life-threatening condition. After returning home, she trained as a community prevention specialist and became certified to perform HIV testing and counseling.

In 2004, Fantashia founded an organization called Heaven Sent Charities, which collects and delivers supplies to HIV-infected orphans in Africa. In addition to dispensing basic staples and medical supplies, she makes a point of also sending teddy bears as a token of love. "It tells them that they're not forgotten," she says.

Fantashia remembers the moment when Henry told her that he was proud of her. It was at a reunion for Bloch Scholars. His words of encouragement cheered her on. And so did the recognition by the Metropolitan Community Colleges; they inducted her into their Hall of Fame.

There are numerous heartwarming stories about the Henry W. Bloch Scholars. A final one: Miguel Pineda's parents emigrated from El Salvador when he was two years old. Unlike his high-school friends who joined a gang, he stayed out of trouble. "My parents have always been in my ear," he says.

Miguel became part of the Bloch Scholars program at Donnelly College in Kansas City, Kansas. "I was the first from both sides of my family to attend and graduate from college," he says. His parents framed his diploma and hung it in their living room. "You can't miss it."

By volunteering at hospitals and health clinics, Miguel, who received his Bachelor of Science degree in biology, discovered that Spanish-speaking patients often don't have access to Spanish-speaking doctors. His goal is to become an osteopathic physician in the Hispanic community.

Miguel wrote Henry a letter of thanks. "He opened a door for me and gave me an opportunity to excel in a way that I never would have had," he says. That opportunity has also helped Miguel's nephews, nieces, and cousins from Los Angeles to New York City. "They didn't see college in their future until they came to my graduation."

Miguel's two sisters clean houses. "They're overwhelmed with joy that I finished college," he says. "And they're happy that their children have a role model."

With more and more Henry W. Bloch Scholar graduates joining the workforce, the foundation is developing a mechanism to track their success. Meanwhile, Henry continues to take immense pleasure in meeting and getting to know the new students each semester. "Our foundation would be hard-pressed to find a better use of its money," he says.

A Debt to Society

"This is not a world we can turn our backs on," Henry said in a commencement address. "We cannot retreat into our own private worlds, into our personal castles, pulling the drawbridge in behind us. There is no safe place where we can shrug our shoulders and say, 'But it doesn't concern me.' "

Henry didn't turn his back on Kansas City's problems. "The city has been good to me and my family," he says. "I owe a debt to society." He has been working to pay it off for a long time.

In the early 1960s, he started accepting invitations to join boards of local, nonprofit organizations. He quickly found himself getting more than he was giving. "I benefited from serving with other leaders in the community," he says. "I learned from them." Eventually, he led the boards of several of those organizations—including Midwest Research Institute, the Civic Council of Greater Kansas City, the UMKC Trustees, the Greater Kansas City Chamber of Commerce, the Heart of America United Way, and the Menorah Medical Foundation, to name a few.

Henry established the H&R Block Foundation in 1974 to ensure that the company would remain a good corporate citizen. More than 35 years later, he continues to serve as its chairman. With the exception of one year, the company has made annual contributions to the foundation, resulting in more than $40 million in total distributions to worthwhile causes and organizations. Most of the charitable support is in four broad areas—arts and culture, community development, education, and health and human services.

Since 2002, David Miles, a former university fundraiser, has been president of the foundation. He is in charge of recommending grants to the board and monitoring the foundation's investments in the community. David and the staff also encourage the company's employees to get personally involved. As the foundation's web site says, "Giving to the community is part of the H&R Block culture. The H&R Block Foundation supports that culture by hosting several programs that encourage and recognize the participation of associates who help improve the communities where they live and work." Through its Cash for Champions program, for example, nonprofit organizations at which Block associates volunteer can receive financial aid from the foundation. In addition to the Henry Bloch Scholars program, the foundation grants between 150 and 200 college scholarships annually to children of company associates.

The foundation's work cuts across the giving continuum. At one end, there are charitable donations for basic human services. At the other end, there are investments to change society. The Henry W. Bloch Scholars program is an example of the latter.

"Henry doesn't use the foundation to support his favorite causes," David says. "He empowers the staff to do its independent research and make its own recommendations to the board. He insists on precision and truthfulness. He has helped me grow tremendously."

Upon Henry's retirement from the H&R Block board in 2000, the foundation wanted to do something beyond establishing the scholarship program in his name. Fellow board member and civic leader Morton Sosland had an idea. Kansas Citians have long been proud that their home-town ranks second only to Rome as the city with the most fountains. But there was no fountain named after one of its most renowned citizens.

In 2001, the *New York Times* described the city's newest and argu-ably most spectacular fountain. "All summer long and well into autumn, water shoots, gurgles and dances amid light and sculpture from the more than 100 fountains of Kansas City. They were first built over natural springs more than a century ago to provide water for the city's 70,000 horses. The tradition flourished to the point that today almost any major public or private construction project has to include a fountain. . . . One of the newest is the Henry W. Bloch Fountain, dedicated last year in front of the restored Union Station. With jets of

The Henry Wollman Bloch Fountain
Courtesy of Brian Bloch.

water pumped through 232 nozzles, the Bloch Fountain is programmed to display vertical water designs shooting as high as 120 feet."[3]

Like the Bloch Scholars program and the Bloch School, the initial planning for the Bloch Fountain was kept a secret from Henry. After Morton presented the drawings to him, Henry was excited about the foundation's magnificent gift to the city.

Kansas City has been good to Henry Bloch and H&R Block. He and the Block Foundation are returning the favor.

HENRY'S DEDUCTIONS

- A commitment to the greater good is good business.
- Make giving back part of your corporate culture.
- Encourage your associates to get involved in their communities.

Chapter 18

Making an Impression

H enry's personal philanthropic legacy includes generous support of the Nelson-Atkins Museum of Art, which houses one of the finest art collections in the country. For three years Henry served as chairman of the Kansas City museum's board of trustees. In preparation for the twenty-first century, he and the board embarked on a plan to expand the facility by more than half. A team oversaw an international competition for the design of the addition, which would be named the Bloch Building.

The group embraced architect Steven Holl's concept to build five freestanding, translucent glass pavilions or "lenses" cascading down the side of a hill. A series of underground galleries would be linked to the lenses. During the day, natural light would reflect into the galleries. At night, gallery lights would permeate the 16-inch glass panels of each lens. Henry was impressed with the dramatic, artistic, and provocative design. But the plan sparked considerable controversy.

"It is grotesque!" someone said. "The lenses look like giant shipping containers!" another remarked. Letters to the editor of the local newspaper mocked the plan. How could Henry Bloch possibly get tricked into supporting such a dreadful design? Henry heard an earful of grumbling. But the experts assured him that the building would be magnificent. Henry maintained his faith in Holl and his team.

Chris McVoy, principal architect with Holl's firm, was well aware of the controversy. "During construction, the design sparked a debate within the community as to the 'appropriateness' of placing such unconventional architecture next to the sacred icon of the city," he said. "The debate spanned the full range of praise and criticism, eliciting comments from people who normally wouldn't give architecture the time of day."[1]

There were also concerns about structural elements of the building. Henry chaired the building committee. "We were doing things with steel and glass that had never been done before," retired museum director and CEO Marc Wilson says. "The engineering that went into this building was unbelievably complicated, sophisticated, and innovative." The museum leadership, the contractor, and the architects each felt compelled to hire their own glass engineer. And Henry felt a duty to weigh the conflicting opinions. As Marc says, "Henry is very deliberate. He does his homework." Assuming the structure wouldn't collapse, there was no question that it represented a terrific architectural and engineering breakthrough.

Marc reflected on the 165,000 square foot, $95 million Bloch Building: "[It] has no facade, no back, not even a face that governs general orientation. It reads not as a single mass but as large, irregular glass-sculptures with variable, shifting visual aspects that deny a quick, easy identification of relationships and function. As you attempt to sort out what you see, no shape lets you infer what lies on its other side. Have you ever been invited by a building to have an active, flowing, three-dimensional relationship with it?"[2]

The Bloch Building opened in 2007 to raves. *Time* ranked the structure as the number-one architectural marvel that year. The *New Yorker* called the Bloch Building "one of the best museums of the last generation" and "as striking and inventive a piece of architectural form . . . and yet it is a serene and exhilarating place in which to view art." The *Chicago Tribune* said, "Not since Frank Gehry's startling eruption

The Bloch Building at the Nelson–Atkins Museum of Art

of metal, the Guggenheim in Bilbao, Spain, made its smashing debut 10 years ago has a museum been this enchanting."

There is much more to the Bloch legacy at the Nelson-Atkins Museum than the striking new building. Marion and Henry have amassed one of the finest private collections of Impressionist and Post-Impressionist paintings in the world. They will leave their incredible collection to the museum.

"Impressionism not only changed the world of art, it had a profound affect on human civilization," Marc says. "Any museum in the world would be thrilled to hang the Blochs' pieces on its walls."

In a listing of the top 100 collectors who have made a difference, *Art & Antiques* described the Blochs' works:

> Marion and Henry Bloch's collection of French paintings is the culmination of serious research, careful deliberation and extensive consultation with conservators and curators, which explains why any one of their 25 masterpieces is worthy of a world-class museum. Highlights include an early version of the Metropolitan Museum of Art's "The Croquet Party" by Manet, "Restaurant Rispal at Asnières" by van Gogh, "The Willow" by Gauguin (from his Pont Aven period) and "Bibemus Quarry" and "The Pipe Smoker" by Cézanne. Other outstanding paintings are

Marion's favorite work
in the collection is Pierre
Bonnard's *The White
Cupboard*

by Bonnard, Seurat, Matisse, Monet, Pissarro and Sisley. What unites all these works is consistent high quality and what Nelson-Atkins Museum of Art curator Ian Kennedy calls "a very personal touch, similar to the Ailsa Mellon Bruce paintings at the National Gallery in Washington, D.C."[3]

The first public display of the Blochs' collection was at a special exhibit inaugurating the Bloch Building. Marion and Henry also loaned a painting that was not part of their Impressionist collection—a stunning 1975 portrait of Marion by Andy Warhol. The artist actually created four portraits of her, each with a different colored background. The Blochs kept one and gave one to the Nelson-Atkins. The other two reside at the Andy Warhol Museum in Pittsburgh. The four portraits were displayed together for the first time at the opening.

The Blochs began collecting art in the 1970s for the most mundane of reasons. "When we built our house, we wanted pretty pictures on the wall," Henry says. On a family vacation, they browsed galleries in Amsterdam and purchased a painting by seventeenth-century Dutch artist, Isaac van Ostade.

"I had it sent to the Nelson," Henry says. "When we got home, the conservator told me it might have been painted by him at one time, but the work had been completely repainted. It really had no value." From that point, Henry relied on experts before making art acquisitions. As his net worth grew, he decided in 1976 to upgrade to French Impressionism. That's when he began counting on the expertise of Ted Coe, the retired director of the Nelson-Atkins. He and Marion never envisioned buying as many great works as they did. "Once we started, it was hard to stop."

"I never intended to sell the paintings," Henry says. "Besides, I always thought I had paid too much. As it turned out, I couldn't afford any of them today." He is pleased that the works will be permanently housed at the Nelson-Atkins. "I think the paintings are lonely in our house. They'll be much happier in the museum."

Marc speaks about his long relationship with Henry. "He is one of the most thoroughly decent people I've ever met or worked with, a man of tremendous integrity. He is shy and modest, never wanting to call attention to himself. Henry doesn't mind appreciation, but he doesn't want his name emblazoned on the front page of the newspaper.

In working with him, you may have to work out differences of opinion, but you never have to watch your back."

With the addition of the Bloch Building and the promised gift of the Blochs' Impressionist collection, Henry and Marion's legacy will benefit the lives of millions of people for generations.

Giving Back

For Henry, giving does not mean "blank-check" charity. He wants to be personally engaged and strategic in his social investments. "I get more bang for the buck when I am personally involved," he says. He stays in regular communication with the dean of the Bloch School and the executive director of the Nelson-Atkins Museum. They seek his advice and guidance. As David Miles says, "Henry is very focused. He has clear objectives, he demands the best, and he rewards people for good performance."

David describes Henry as more than a social entrepreneur. "He's one of the individuals who invented social entrepreneurship," David says. "He brought his business talents to the community and to social issues in order to create positive change. Kansas City has been rewarded immensely from his talent and generosity."

As a business entrepreneur, Henry measured success based on the company's annual growth in market share and profits. But as a social entrepreneur, he has a less objective measuring stick. "How has my investment of time and/or money benefited society?" he asks.

"H&R Block is *for-profit*," he explains. "The business school, the scholarship program, the museum addition, and our art collection—these are *more-than-profit*."

"It's important for everyone, regardless of financial capacity, to give back," Henry says. "Don't put off getting involved because you don't believe you have time. Giving back, even in the smallest way, can make a big difference."

"Giving is individual," he continues. "Find something you're interested in, something you enjoy. But understand that giving is also about receiving."

"Not everyone gets it," he says. "I have some friends who don't want to be involved. They don't give time or money. Frankly, I feel sorry for them. They don't know the genuine pleasure that comes from giving."

Henry offered this advice to new college graduates: "Be thoughtful and active citizens of your communities. Live your lives to the fullest, for we pass this way only once. Remember that life cannot be aimless, but must be purposeful, and freedom does not mean freedom from responsibility but freedom to work and to accomplish. You will find that true success is not measured in what you take away but in what you give. Paradoxically, the more you give, the more you will take away."

"Henry Bloch is one of the most special individuals that Kansas City has ever had—one of the kindest, most caring and wisest," David Miles says. "But it's the purity of his heart that I admire the most. He has had an incredible dedication to the community for so many years—and he's still at it every day."

"Some of that has to do with the way Henry grew up," Ed Matheny explains. "He was raised to not only take care of himself and his loved ones but to also be a contributing member of society. That's Henry in spades."

"I don't know another corporate executive in another city that has reflected the responsibility and leadership toward his community to the degree that Henry has," Morton Sosland says. "Henry has loved the role, and his response to loving it has been to do it very well."

"It's not a chore to pay off this debt to society," Henry says. "It's a pleasure. And money is only part of it."

Henry's Deductions

- When you have three meals a day, it's time to help the next person.
- True success is not measured in what you get, but in what you give back.
- When you give, you receive much more.

Chapter 19

And Then Some

During a Q&A session with entrepreneurship students at the University of Missouri-Kansas City (UMKC), Henry was asked what separates an entrepreneur from a businessperson. He responded with one of his favorite jokes.

"There is a strip shopping center with three stores, each selling the same general merchandise at the same general price," he begins. "The manager at one end of the center places a sign in the window, saying YEAR-END SALE! At the other end, the store manager hangs a sign that reads, GOING OUT OF BUSINESS SALE! An entrepreneur runs the store in the middle. What message does he put on his sign? MAIN ENTRANCE."

Is it possible to teach students how to think and act like an entrepreneur? Academic leaders at the Henry W. Bloch School of Business and Public Administration at UMKC believe it is possible—and they are proving it. The School's nationally recognized Institute for Entrepreneurship and Innovation (IEI) has created a paradigm shift in business education through a combination of transformational research and experiential learning.

Decades ago, naysayers argued that basic management and strategy could not be taught. Pointing to some of the great business icons who didn't even attend college, they claimed you either had these innate skills or you didn't. Now that college courses in management and strategy are ubiquitous, the legitimacy of these academic disciplines is rarely ever questioned.

The study of entrepreneurship is on a similar track. Doubters are questioning whether this relatively new field in higher education is a legitimate area of academic study. But the Bloch School's dean, Dr. Teng-Kee Tan, contends that it is imperative to develop an entrepreneurial mindset.

"We must teach people to think in new ways," he says, "and we must take entrepreneurship across all disciplines, making it accessible to everyone."

At UMKC, all undergraduate business students are required to take a capstone entrepreneurship class. They must plan, incubate, and manage a new venture in a simulated environment. Graduate students go one step further by launching their ventures in the real world.

Tencap Tennis is one of many new ventures conceived and implemented by Bloch School graduates. The company sells a rating system for tennis clubs and leagues. Another new product incubated at the IEI is Prêt-à-Yoga, a portable yoga application for the Apple iPhone and iPod Touch. There's Zoom IM, a company that develops marketing campaigns to attract and retain customers through personalized messages. And one more example is BioRich Products, which provides organically reconstituted soil additives to farmers to help them increase their crop yield while reducing application frequency.

Through the IEI's Venture Creation Challenge, the Bloch School expects to produce 100 entrepreneurs and 10 high-growth ventures annually. Considering that the average entrepreneur creates over 500 jobs, the potential economic impact of this program is significant.

The IEI has assembled one of the largest and most talented entrepreneurship faculties anywhere. Its founder and executive director,

At the Venture Creation Challenge, IEI students present new concepts to local investors and entrepreneurs

Dr. Michael Song, is recognized as the world's foremost innovation management scholar. Why would the top-ranked researcher in his field choose to come to the Bloch School?

"The tipping point was my meeting with Henry Bloch," Michael explains. "He told me that he had always believed in doing his best at whatever he undertook. I knew he was serious about wanting the Bloch School to be one of the very best." Michael also knew that Henry gave more than money to the Bloch School; he lectures in the classroom and spends time meeting with students. "He has been an inspiration to all of us."

Unlike conventional business schools that focus on efficiency, the IEI concentrates on value creation. Budding entrepreneurs are exposed to everything it takes to start and operate a company—business planning, budgeting, hiring, marketing, and so forth. They hear "war stories" from other entrepreneurs. And they are given an opportunity to apply theory to the real world by creating new products and services.

"Starting a venture helps students develop confidence," Michael says. "This is important because people often tend to back away from new business opportunities if they lack experience."

Not all graduates of the IEI are expected to start their own companies from scratch. Many of them will become intrapreneurs—innovators who work within established companies. Michael and his longtime research partner, Dr. Mark Perry, have explored how large companies can create a competitive advantage through venture creation. It starts with identifying and selecting individuals with the right entrepreneurial skills and experiences.

Like many entrepreneurs from past generations, Henry never had an opportunity to receive a formal entrepreneurship education. He learned the old fashioned way—trial and error.

"If the IEI had existed when I attended college, it may have helped me avoid some of my early mistakes," he says. "I was lucky that I succeeded. My hope is that the failure rate of new businesses started by the next generation of entrepreneurs who train at the IEI will be lower than the national average."

When Henry is asked to share his hard-won lessons to IEI students, he often begins with one of his favorite expressions: "And then some."

"The person who succeeds is the one who does his or her own job, and then some; who is thoughtful to others, and then some; who meets obligations and responsibilities, and then some," Henry explains. "That's the person who steps ahead of the crowd and goes on to great heights."[1]

Here are some tips that Henry offers budding entrepreneurs.

Secrets of the Successful Entrepreneur

Find your calling and follow your heart. As Henry once told Walter Cronkite, "I always wanted to do something different, something more than just a job, something to contribute to society." He discovered that personal fulfillment doesn't come from money or power. "When you are passionate about your vocation or avocation, your life has purpose."

There is no substitute for hard work. Henry developed a strong work ethic before he started his business. To make passing grades in school, he had to work hard. "There are no shortcuts," he says.

Persevere. Successful entrepreneurs like Henry credit their success to an unwillingness to surrender. They are pigheaded and resilient, sticking with their goal in the face of obstacles and setbacks. They believe in themselves and their work, even when doubters advise them to quit. Henry, who persevered for eight years before finally achieving success, didn't lose faith. "I never thought about failing," he says.

Someone said, "Success is largely a matter of holding on after others let go." Or as Albert Einstein put it, "When you're going through hell, keep on going."

Have fun. "It's difficult to be successful unless you enjoy what you're doing," Henry says. The brothers found tremendous pleasure in doing taxes for others.

Dick once said, "My greatest joy in life is to do tax returns . . . Love 'em!"[2]

"It's contagious," Henry says. When employees realize that the boss is having fun, they are more inclined to be happy in their jobs.

Pay attention to details. "The difference between success and failure is usually in the little things," Henry says. In training sessions with Block field managers, he urged them to take pride in every element of the operation. "If the sign in your window is crooked," Henry often said, "then other things in your office are wrong."

Bad breaks can be good. "Look for an opportunity in every challenge," Henry says.

An avid bridge player, he learned that being dealt a poor hand doesn't necessarily mean that you can't win. Throughout the years, the brothers were dealt plenty of bad hands. Early on, attorneys and CPAs charged that the company engaged in unfair competition. Threats of regulatory actions made Henry plenty nervous. Hoping to find more hospitable regulatory environments, he and Dick rapidly opened offices in other states. What appeared at the time to be a bad break triggered a speedy expansion. Being the first to market helped cement H&R Block's dominant position in the retail tax market.

Believe in luck. Henry is a huge believer in luck. There is an important distinction, however, between chance and luck. With chance, you have no control over the outcome. With luck, you have something to do with the result. Although Henry can rattle off one lucky break after another, in every case good fortune was more than a random act. Louis Pasteur, one of Henry's childhood idols, said, "Luck favors the prepared mind."

In H&R Block's first year, the IRS decided to stop preparing taxes for free in its Kansas City offices. This proved to be a boon for the Blochs' novel experiment. "It was pure luck," Henry says. But there is no escaping the fact that he and Dick were prepared to seize on the opportunity; they positioned themselves in the right place at the right time.

Fail small. "Success is often the product of past failures," Henry says. But entrepreneurs who "bet the ranch" and then lose the ranch may not have another chance to succeed. This may help explain why one-third of small businesses fail within their first two years and about half go out of business within five years. To reduce the chance of business failure, test new ideas on a small scale and learn from any mistakes.

Listen to your gut. Henry's intuition played an important role in his decision-making process. But he didn't let his hunches or "inner voice" outweigh hard facts, research, or reason.

Balance your act. "Achieving a balance between your professional and personal life helps you *and* your company," Henry says. He had five priorities—family, work, community, sports, and vacation. Although he did his best to make time for each, he found that it is not easy for hard-working entrepreneurs to achieve equilibrium.

Building the Winning Team

Surround yourself with the best people. "People are the most valuable asset in any company," Henry says. That's why he tried to hire individuals who were smarter than him.

Former Block board member Morton Sosland says, "In my mind, nothing reflects more favorably on Henry than his ability to single out people who are capable and let them carry forward."

Develop teamwork. "Every business is a people business," Henry says. Healthy relationships and collaboration are a hallmark of successful companies. Henry encouraged individuals, groups, and departments to work closely together. He made sure that when goals were met, they celebrated success.

In the middle of the tax season, every district manager hosted an annual banquet for all seasonal tax office associates and their spouses. "It was a tradition that fostered teamwork and showed the staff that their contributions and hard work were valued," Henry says.

Give credit where credit is due. "Notice when others have great ideas and give them credit," Henry says. "This encourages them to come up with more ideas." Henry, whose style was to deflect praise, has a natural gift for acknowledging the contributions of others. For example, he never fails to give credit for his big break in business to John White, the advertising salesman with the Kansas City newspaper who approached the brothers about placing an ad for tax preparation in 1955.

"To this day, when Henry talks about the founding of H&R Block," John says, "he mentions my name."

Remember the Golden Rule. "Don't let success go to your head," Henry warns. Just because you're the boss doesn't mean you are superior.

Hold yourself and others accountable. "Good leaders follow through, follow up, and set an example for others," Henry says.

The boss who worries about being everyone's friend will be liked—but not respected. Henry monitored his own performance as well as the performance of each person who reported directly to him. "Every business goal should have a champion," he says, "and the champion should be an individual, not a committee."

Reward good performance. "Pay-for-performance is a motivator," Henry says. While helping retain top talent, it also aligns the associates' activities with the company's strategic plan. Developing performance goals is both an art and a science. At Block, the metrics usually consisted of financial and non-financial indicators that were consistent with shareholder interests. "Pay-for-performance is an incentive for top performers, and it helps weed out bottom performers."

Set aggressive goals that your team can embrace. Yogi Berra said, "If you don't set goals, you can't regret not reaching them." But Henry points out that setting goals isn't enough; there must be buy-in of the goals throughout the organization. This requires clear communication, regular tracking of results along the way, and continually keeping the goals on top of the associates' minds.

In 1965, Henry publicly announced his audacious goal to prepare 10 percent of the nation's returns. At the time, Block was serving less than three percent of all taxpayers. Thanks to a mammoth team-wide effort, Block achieved that goal nine years later.

Keep an open door policy. Morale and productivity are enhanced when senior managers are accessible to subordinates. "It is amazing how problems can develop when there is a lack of open communication," Henry says. Employee forums can foster a healthy internal dialogue. Use of technology can also enhance a company's ability to keep associates connected and informed in a timely manner.

Thriving in the Changing Marketplace

Don't underestimate the power of low prices. "In the early days of the company, one of our board members told me, 'You won't be able to make much money by charging only $5 for a tax return.'" But Henry discovered that low prices, coupled with low costs and high quality, make for an unbeatable—and profitable—combination. "There's no better way to stimulate demand, achieve economies of scale, create a competitive advantage, and gain market share."

Specialize, customize, and individualize. In the mid-1940s, Henry and his brother Leon began their business by marketing 50 services. "That approach makes no sense in this era of specialization," Henry says. "Consumers want choices, and they demand products that satisfy their individual needs." To attract an increasingly discriminating and sophisticated consumer, H&R Block has tried to target products and services to taxpayer segments using a combination of online and retail offerings.

Make technology a strategic weapon. "Anticipate how technology can produce a unique advantage for your business," Henry says. In the late 1980s, H&R Block was among the first in its industry to computerize the tax preparation process and offer electronic filing at its stores. These developments revolutionized the business; product quality improved appreciably and the turnaround time for tax refunds was significantly reduced.

But today, the industry landscape is noticeably different in terms of competitive dynamics and technology. H&R Block, like most companies, is facing substantial opportunities and acute threats vis-à-vis the growing use of the Internet. How should Block and other brick-and-mortar tax firms deal with the ever-increasing use by taxpayers of inexpensive and easy-to-use online tax preparation offerings? Will the Internet eventually make the retail offices outmoded?

These types of questions aren't unique to the tax industry. "More and more consumers are embracing the Internet in place of traditional stores," Henry says. "It's a phenomenon that won't go away. Companies must respond, or they risk obsolescence."

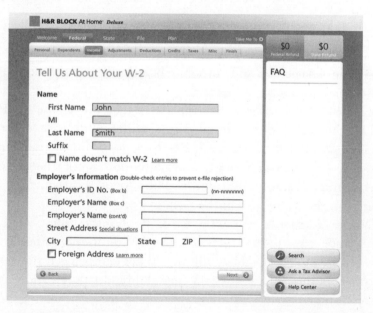

H&R Block At Home allows taxpayers to complete and file their returns using a personal computer

Customers are always right, even when they are wrong. "A customer who complains represents an opportunity to gain a customer for life," Henry says. "Stress courtesy and humility with everyone you come in contact." Research shows that for every unsatisfied customer who complains, at least two dozen don't. Likewise, an unsatisfied customer tells at least eight others about his or her bad experience.

Promote a diversity of thinking and talent. "Urge associates to express their ideas, even if their thoughts are contradictory to yours or the majority view," Henry says. He knows that some of the best ideas come from individuals who think outside the box. A diverse workforce—in terms of cultural backgrounds, gender, lifestyles, color, and age—adds rich perspectives.

Improve yourself. Complacency ultimately leads to excuses and failure. Endeavor to become a better manager, leader, and person. Continually raise personal and professional standards through self-evaluation and feedback from others. But don't confuse improvement with perfection. "Everyone can do better," Henry says. "Don't put off addressing your weaknesses. They will not dissolve of their own accord."

Find a mentor. "No one has all the answers," Henry says. "Reach out to individuals you respect for advice and counsel." When Henry joined civic, charitable, and corporate boards, he eagerly learned from other experienced business leaders.

Execute. "It is easier to develop a plan than to execute it," Henry says. The best-laid plans are worthless without effective execution. Although traditional business schools do a good job of teaching students how to develop strategy, more attention should be placed on implementing strategy. "Execution boils down to having the right people with the right skills in the right place."

Don't demand respect—earn it. Some bosses think they deserve respect because of their title or position in the corporate hierarchy. Henry disagrees. "The only way to get true respect is to earn it," he says. "Take the blame for your mistakes and failures, show respect to others, and be sincere. And always keep your commitments."

Creating a Responsible and Dynamic Business

Build a strong culture. Every company has a distinct culture and a set of written or unwritten core values. The best way to get a sense of these qualities is from talking to employees. A corporate culture should create a powerful, positive energy that permeates the entire organization.

Henry and Dick made sure that frugality was a central element of Block's culture. "We explained to our associates that keeping expenses low would translate into keeping prices low," Henry says. "This allowed us to refrain from raising prices during our first 12 years. Associates embraced our way of doing business because it was in the best interest of customers."

Avoid rubber-stamp boards: "When a board operates like a clique, it's a sign of bad corporate governance," Henry says. "Good directors are independent thinkers. They ask tough questions, demand answers and, if necessary, blow whistles."

When he was CEO, Henry appreciated it when board members challenged and even disagreed with him. He even encouraged it. "When the board of a company automatically goes along with the chairman or CEO's suggestions," he says, "the directors don't add value, and they do a disservice to shareholders."

Concentrate on your core competency. In the 1970s, H&R Block began acquiring businesses. In many cases, there was no strategic fit between the acquired companies and the core tax business. Although some of the purchases worked out well, others did not. Diversification, Henry concluded, makes sense if it is synergistic and management understands how to run the new business. "But the odds are not good," Henry warns. "Most acquisitions fail to achieve their anticipated value."

Value your name. Henry always stressed that ethical behavior was an absolute imperative within the company. In an era rife with corporate scandals, the importance of communicating and reinforcing a code of ethics has never been greater. "Always be honest with yourself and with others," Henry says. "Your reputation and your company's reputation can be permanently damaged by a single unethical decision."

With his name on the door, Henry always felt that if H&R Block's reputation was tarnished, his own standing was impaired. Quoting Shakespeare, Henry says: "Who steals my purse steals trash . . . but he that filches from me my good name robs me of that which not enriches him and makes me poor indeed."

Keep debt to a minimum. "A man in debt is so far a slave." This Ralph Waldo Emerson quote is one of Henry's favorites.

Henry attempted to avoid debt personally and in business. He believes that, sooner or later, every company will stumble or face tough economic times. "The organization that maintains a strong balance sheet is more likely to survive a downturn or strike opportunistically during a down cycle," Henry says. "Remember, cash is king!"

There's no place for greed. During H&R Block's expansion phase, the board of directors tried repeatedly to increase Henry and Dick's compensation. But the brothers turned them down. Both men were living comfortably and figured that the company could put the extra money to good use. Entrepreneurs who start a business for purely materialistic reasons are less likely to achieve success. "There is a big difference between drive and greed," Henry says. "Drive furthers a company's mission while greed impedes it."

Focus on long-term value creation. "I sometimes wonder if H&R Block would be better off today if it had never become a public company," Henry says. "Too many executives of public companies bow to the intense pressure from analysts and short-term oriented shareholders to deliver short-term results. This puts long-term growth at greater risk."

Henry is opposed to the common practice among public companies of issuing quarterly or even annual earnings guidance to investors. "Providing guidance, especially for a seasonal business like tax preparation, adds further pressure on management to focus on near-term success," Henry says. He isn't the only one who is concerned about the pervasive short-term orientation among American corporations.

A group of 28 prominent investors, academicians, and business leaders, including Warren Buffett and former IBM CEO Louis Gerstner, released this statement: "We believe that short-term objectives have eroded faith in corporations continuing to be the foundation of the American free enterprise system, which has been, in turn, the foundation of our economy." One solution to this problem, which Henry supports, is to require investors to hold shares of stock for longer time periods in order to qualify for the capital gains rate.[3]

Be socially responsible. "Every company should behave responsibly and be concerned about the larger society," Henry says. The H&R

Block Foundation, which Henry founded, continues the company's legacy of investing in and enriching Kansas City and the communities in which Block associates live.

In addition to supporting civic initiatives, businesses should be stewards of the environment. It's not only the right thing to do, but environmental stewardship also endears employees and customers to the company, resulting in a higher brand perception. "As our global society faces unprecedented challenges," Henry says, "a commitment to the greater good is a necessary business strategy."

Continually adapt your plans. "To help any business stay a step ahead of the competition, strategic planning is crucial," Henry says. Ideally, it provides a roadmap developed through a collaborative process. "When it comes to planning, flexibility is more important than formality." Managers must always be prepared to adjust their plans based on internal and external circumstances. "Change is inevitable. Get on with it without delay."

Stay lean. During Henry's years at the company, H&R Block was lean, if not short-handed. As Henry says, "It is better for a staff to be challenged with too much work than not enough to keep them busy." Employees are also happier when they feel challenged. "The firm that acts big and bureaucratic is at a serious competitive disadvantage."

True Success

For Henry, becoming an entrepreneur was more than a career decision—it was a way of life. Although there were plenty of ups and downs at the outset, he achieved his initial goal of being his own boss. He beat the odds—and then some.

In the classroom and through experiential education, the faculty at the Bloch School's IEI is helping others pursue that same way of life. Their ultimate goal is to reduce the staggeringly high failure rate of new businesses. Early results demonstrate that entrepreneurship education is a legitimate, even indispensable field of study. Market-ready entrepreneurs who have successfully completed the IEI program seem to be accelerating the pace of social and economic development.

Henry trusts that this new wave of entrepreneurs won't merely gauge their success on the size of the companies they build, the fortunes they amass, or the fame they achieve. True success, he stresses, is rooted in two fundamental questions: Are you doing what you love, and are you leaving the world a better place?

HENRY'S DEDUCTIONS

- In business and in life, act with purpose and evidence good character.
- Constantly strive to improve. Everything is temporary— including success.
- Give more of yourself than is expected.

Chapter 20

Miscellaneous Deductions

Henry marched up the four flights of stairs to his office. Until recently, he would never have held onto the railing. As he ascended the steps, he contemplated whether or not to attend the Kansas City Chiefs' football game on the following Sunday. The weatherman was predicting frigid temperatures for the kickoff. A season ticket holder since the team was founded in 1960, he finally decided to watch the game on TV at his home. Until recently, he would never have missed cheering on the home team in person.

Although he approaches his daily activities with more caution than when he was younger, some things haven't changed. Among them is the same old unshakable feeling that there is so much more to be accomplished.

"I'd be bored living a life of leisure," Henry says. "It's important to feel useful." Keeping busy is a lesson he learned from one of his first mentors, Arthur Mag, who was Harry Truman's legal counsel and one of Kansas City's most prominent civic leaders.

"Stay active," Arthur ordered Henry. "Never retire." Until the day he died in 1981, Mag practiced what he preached.

"The days of our years are threescore years and ten," Henry says, quoting the Bible. That's 70 years. "I feel very fortunate. I'm 88, and I really don't feel old."

Though he isn't as spry as he used to be, Henry's energy level remains exceptional. It's a good thing because he is dealing with a most difficult challenge—Marion's declining health. He has had plenty of experience tackling and overcoming problems, but luck doesn't seem to be on his side this time. Yet he takes on this setback with all the vigor and determination anyone could muster.

Before the football kickoff that Sunday morning, Dr. John Helzberg comes over to the Blochs' home to see Marion.

"Big breath!" John instructs his patient while listening to her heart and lungs through his stethoscope. "Real big breath!" Seconds later, Marion complies. "Oh, that's perfect."

Marion looks comfortable in her recliner chair, a warm blanket enveloping her weakened body. At 80 years old, she is still beautiful. Her sentences are short and her voice is faint, but she still manages to show the same loving smile that never fails to raise Henry's spirits. Marion requires 24-hour care because she is dependent in all activities of daily living. Amazingly, she never complains.

She gives John the same smile that endears him and everyone else to her. He is her doctor—and also her nephew. Besides making regular house calls to check on her status, he talks to Henry at least twice a day, every day.

"I would do anything for Aunt Marion," the Yale-trained gastroenterologist says. His father Jim Helzberg was Marion's older brother and a close friend of Henry's. Jim fixed the couple up on their first date.

On this routine checkup, John asks her to squeeze his hand. He wants to know that she still has muscle reflex control. After repeating the question more slowly, she squeezes—not once but twice.

"Squeezing two times is an old Helzberg sign," John says. "It means 'I love you.' My dad passed it on to me." Marion passed it on to her children.

At 8 o'clock each morning and evening, Henry takes Marion's blood pressure, pulse, oxygen saturation, and temperature. After jotting down the vital signs in a log, he compares the readings with the numbers he entered 12 hours earlier, noting any trends. Then he phones John, who uses the data to determine whether her next round of medicines should be adjusted. "Our number-one priority is to keep her at home, seizure-free and pain-free," John says.

Marion has been free of cancer for over 20 years. Even more remarkable, as John notes, it is extremely rare for anyone subjected to radiation therapy on the brain to survive that long. "Her current condition is caused by a decrease of blood flow to the brain," he explains. "But it's a miracle that she is alive."

Henry remembers how thrilled he was when Marion reached her five-year anniversary of being cancer free. It was back in 1993, and Henry threw an elegant dinner party at their home. The invitation list was short; it included the couple's four children and their spouses. One of Kansas City's premiere caterers brought out the couple's linen, china, crystal, and silver, which accentuated the gorgeously prepared multicourse dinner and exceptional French wine. Uncharacteristically, Henry had gone to a liquor store where he asked the owner for his finest bottle of red wine. It was an exquisite, unforgettable celebration.

John and Henry give each other the credit for Marion's prolonged life. "I don't think she'd still be with us if it weren't for John," Henry says. "I couldn't be more grateful." Henry is also grateful to Marion's exceptional caregivers, especially Carrie Cameron, who looks after her as if Marion were her own mother.

Henry wanted to do something to show his gratitude to John. But John refused payment for the medical care he supplied Marion, not to mention the attention and support he provided Henry. So Henry made arrangements to endow a professorship in medicine at the University of Missouri-Kansas City in John's honor. John asked, however, that the position be named not for himself but for his Aunt Marion.

Henry's close friends and relatives have been in awe of his continuous and intensely compassionate attentiveness toward Marion during her long, debilitating illness.

"What a great love affair," Marion's cousin Charles Helzberg says. "Always has been."

Friend Ed Matheny agrees: "The great affection is still there."

Henry reveals the secret to their special marriage: "It's simple. Do what your spouse wants. I always wanted to do what Marion wanted, and she always wanted to do what I wanted. Practically the only arguments we ever had were when we both were adamant about doing what the other wanted."

Jack Nachman, a friend for over 75 years and a groomsman in the Blochs' wedding, vouches for the couple's unusually strong bond. "He always puts Marion first." But Jack suggests there's more to it than that. Both Marion and Henry are down-to-earth, uncomplicated, and good-hearted. "The millions of dollars Henry has made mean nothing to either of them. They don't flaunt it and they don't worship it."

A Decent Man

More than seventy years ago, Henry's high school and college friends wouldn't have considered voting for him as the most likely to succeed. "He was more the underdog," one friend says. Maybe that's why Henry, an avid sports fan, has always rooted for the underdog. For 40 years, he and Jack bet $2 on every regular and post-season NFL game. Practically the only time Henry didn't pull for the underdog was when the Kansas City Chiefs were favored—which has been rare in recent years.

Just because Henry may have been an underdog doesn't mean he readily accepted losing. "He was a fierce competitor on the tennis court," Ed says.

"If we had played golf or bridge for a nickel, he would have wanted to win that nickel," Jack says. "And to this day, a nickel is still a nickel to him."

Aristotle said, "Men are divided between those who are as thrifty as if they would live forever, and those who are as extravagant as if they were going to die the next day." Except for splurging on his art collection of Impressionist masters and wonderful summer vacations with his family, Henry was solidly in the former camp.

Henry never cared to live big, nor did he ever get a big head. David Miles, the president of the H&R Block Foundation, tells about walking with Henry through the lobby of H&R Block's headquarters on their way to the cafeteria. An employee approached Henry and asked him for his autograph. After signing his name on the paper, Henry turned to David and asked, "Why would anyone want *my* autograph?"

"It was such a humbling moment," David says. "Henry doesn't realize that when he comes into the headquarters he is a rock star. When he walks through the halls, employees pull out their cell phones to take his picture."

"Henry is just Henry," Jack says. "He hasn't changed a bit."

"You've got to love the guy," Ed says. "He is so humble. Henry doesn't parade around, saying, 'Look at what I've done.' He lets his record speak for itself. He'll leave a legacy of being a decent human being."

To Henry, being decent means doing the right thing. He once found an error on his bank statement—in his favor. "I was paid $2,700 twice on a single transaction." He didn't hesitate to bring the matter to the bank's attention. "I always want to have a clear conscience."

"The IRS can audit my tax returns as long as they want to," he continues. "I enjoy paying my fair share of taxes—it is my duty. And I want to be able to sleep at night."

Henry entrusts others to have a clear conscience, too. He recently hired a bricklayer to replace broken sections of his patio. In the middle of the project, the workman asked Henry for a partial payment. He explained that his children needed back-to-school supplies, and he was short of money. Instead of paying the man half, Henry gave him a check for the full amount.

"I had faith that he would come back and finish the project," Henry says. "But if I was wrong and he didn't return, he would have been the bigger loser."

When Henry was in college and then in the war, he occasionally wrote his brothers and his parents. His letters portray a confident, maturing young man finding the meaning of life. In one letter, the University of Michigan student congratulated his younger brother Dick on his birthday. Here is an excerpt:

> It's a funny thing about birthdays: when you are young they seem to be wonderful. In fact nothing is better than to get lots

of presents and know that you are growing into manhood. You ignore your past and the many mistakes, and cheerfully look forward. In later years, however, birthdays just denote the passing of time; instead of opening the future, they suggest the past. It is then that you wonder if your life has been as you hoped it would when you were a boy. You then realize that your future is determined by your past and not by adolescent dreams. It is the same old story that if you live right from day to day your future will take care of itself. Dick, the point I'm trying to stress is that you can only have a happy birthday if your past satisfies your conscience. . . . From this rambling it probably looks as if I am turning into a disciple of Emerson.

Henry doesn't know whether any of his letters influenced his brothers. "You never know when you can have a positive impact on another person—including a complete stranger," he says.

Henry still remembers what a complete stranger said to him in the first month he and Leon started out in business together. A woman who worked in the real estate office where the brothers subleased a cubicle for $50 a month observed his strong work ethic.

"Someday you will be so busy that you won't be able to do everything yourself!" the woman insisted. "You will be *very* successful!" Henry never forgot her words of encouragement.

No one encouraged Henry more than his mother. "She taught me to believe in myself," he says. She also instructed him to do the right thing. "The way I was raised, being on your best behavior was an expectation, not a subject for discussion. If it was under discussion, you had missed the mark."

Henry still feels a deep debt of gratitude to his parents. "Nothing I could put down on paper could possibly come close to expressing all my love and devotion to you and Dad," he wrote her during the war. "Any faults I may have cannot be yours, and any qualities I may possess are through your teachings."

"Mother told me when I was young that you can love too much," Henry says. More than a half-century later, Henry is reminded of those words—daily. He feels the pain that comes from an overabundance of love for his ailing wife.

"I'd rather love too much than not at all," he explains. "Marion is my whole life."

Henry's focus is neither on the past nor the future. He doesn't delight in reminiscing about the old days at H&R Block or in his personal achievements. Nor does he dwell on how he would like to be remembered. He is too busy looking after Marion and making sure that the good fortune that came his way is properly returned to society.

"Tempus fugit," Henry's father frequently reminded his three sons during his latter years. Today, Henry is of the same mind. Time flies.

"It almost seems like yesterday we painted the words INCOME TAX on two pieces of plywood on our parents' driveway," Henry says. In the years that followed, thousands of H&R Block outlets cropped up, and over 500 million returns have been prepared in them. Henry always gave his best, and the best came back to him.

Among the many Emerson teachings that Henry's mother passed along to him is this one: "To laugh often and much; to win the respect of intelligent people and the affection of children; to earn the appreciation of honest critics and endure the betrayal of false friends; to appreciate beauty; to find the best in others; to leave the world a bit better, whether by a healthy child, a garden patch or a redeemed social condition; to know even one life has breathed easier because you have lived. This is to have succeeded."

Henry has succeeded in leaving the world a bit better—and then some.

HENRY'S DEDUCTIONS

- There are no shortcuts.
- Don't bet against the underdog who refuses to quit.
- You're never too old to dream and achieve worthwhile goals.

Notes

Chapter Two Heaven Can Wait

1. Cheryl Chojnacki, "Reflecting on an Amazing Life," *The Daily Herald*, November 11, 2003, 3.

2. Ibid.

3. Ibid.

Chapter Three Three Nobodies with an Idea

1. Sumner Slichter, *Enterprise in Postwar America*, January 1943, 11.

2. Ibid, 12.

3. Ad, *Minneapolis Messenger*, May 28, 1885, 7.

4. Ad, *Minneapolis Messenger*, December 15, 1884, 1.

5. Hugh Pickens, "E.W. Marland's Pioneer Women Models," December 7, 2008, http://knol.google.com/k/hugh-pickens/hugh-pickens-writes-e-w-marlands/hub5zounu2wt/8#.

Chapter Ten Learning to Soar

1. Associated Press, "H&R Block Thrives on Taxes," *Rocky Mountain News*, September 8, 1965, 3D.

2. "Taxes: The Little Man's Friend," *Newsweek*, February 10, 1969, 72.

3. Warren R. Moulds, "H&R Block Is on the Move," *Chicago Today*, March 5, 1970, 53.

Chapter Eleven   Setbacks and Comebacks

1. Marshall Loeb, "Taxpayers Are Sore," *Time*, March 12, 1979, www.time .com/time/magazine/article/0,9171,948453-1,00.html.

2. "IRS Wars against Tax Pros," *Muskogee Daily Phoenix*, January 1973, 20.

3. "The Troubles That Are Taxing H&R Block," *BusinessWeek*, December 1973, 112.

4. "Money to Burn," *Financial Times*, August 1, 1980, 33.

5. James A. Brickley, Sanjog Misra, and R. Lawrence Van Horn, "Contract Duration: Evidence from Franchising," June 21, 2002, p. 179, www.simon .rochester.edu/fac/misra/JLE_CD.pdf.

Chapter Twelve   Heartbroken

1. *Wall Street Journal*, November 14, 1978.

2. Carol E. Curtis, "Life after April 15," *Forbes*, April 13, 1981, 130.

3. "H&R Block: Expanding beyond Taxes for Faster Growth," *BusinessWeek*, December 8, 1980, 76.

4. Dianne Stafford, "Block Branching Out with Legal Clinics," *Kansas City Star*, December 2, 1980, 4D.

5. "Money to Burn," *Financial Times*, August 1, 1980, 33.

6. Eric Auchard, "CompuServe Is Dead, but Everywhere Lives On," Forbes .com, July 7, 2009, www.forbes.com/feeds/afx/2009/07/07/afx6626554.html.

7. "Henry Bloch Talks Taxes, *Money*, February 1981, 44.

Chapter Thirteen   Gains and Losses

1. John Garrity, "An Act of Conscience: Tom Watson Takes a Stand Against Prejudice," *Sports Illustrated*, December 10, 1990, http://sportsillustrated.cnn .com/vault/article/magazine/MAG1136095/2/index.htm.

2. Joyce E. Smith, "H&R Block Executive Steps Down," *Kansas City Star*, August 1, 1992, B3.

3. Kim Foltz, "Son Succeeds Father as H&R Block Chief," *New York Times*, March 18, 1992, D4.

4. Kenneth Gilpen, "H&R Block to Buy Olde for $850 Million in Cash," *New York Times*, September 2, 1999, www.nytimes.com/1999/09/02/business/ h-r-block-to-buy-olde-for-850-million-in-cash.html.

Chapter Fourteen "Block Heads"

1. "Dave Letterman's Top Ten Excuses for H&R Block's Tax Bumble," *Blue Maumau*, February 28, 2006, www.bluemaumau.org/78/dave_lettermans_top_10_excuses_hr_blocks_tax_bumble?quicktabs_2=0&quicktabs_4=1&quicktabs_1=1.

2. Damon Darlin, "H&R Block's Troubles Offer Opportunities for Some," *New York Times*, March 25, 2006, www.nytimes.com/2006/03/25/business/25money.html?ex=1300942800&en=99983d057cc39142&ei=5088&partner=rssnyt&emc=rss.

3. Andrew Leckey, "H&R Block Overtaxed by Blunders, Litigation," *Chicago Tribune*, March 26, 2006. © Tribune Media Service, Inc. All Rights Reserved. Reprinted with permission.

4. "Option One's Dwindling Options," *BusinessWeek*, March 26, 2007, www.businessweek.com/magazine/content/07_13/b4027040.htm.

5. Dan Margolies, "H&R Block Takes Top Honors in Star 50," *Kansas City Star*, May 11, 2009, www.kansascity.com/208/story/1191324.html.

Chapter Fifteen A Fork in the Road

1. H&R Block, "H&R Block Mails Proxy Materials and Letter to All Shareholders," July 31, 2007, www.handrblock.com/press/PrintPreview.jsp?ArticleID=1364.

2. "Breeden Capital Management LLC Announces It Will Nominate Director Slate for H&R Block," *Business Wire*, 27 June 2007, www.allbusiness.com/services/business-services/4542107-1.html.

3. Dan Margolies, "Block's CEO Tells Shareholders the Company Must Do More to Retain Customers," *Kansas City Star*, September 25, 2009, http://webcache.googleusercontent.com/search?q=cache:e9XsCmusnLQJ:www.tradingmarkets.com/.site/news/Stock%2520News/2546980/+russ+smyth+that%27s+why+our+retention+rate+was+68&cd=1&hl=en&ct=clnk&gl=us&client=safari.

4. "IRS Plans to Step Up Tax Preparer Regulation," *WebCPA*, June 4, 2009, http://74.125.95.132/search?q=cache:r5_3AepynhsJ:www.webcpa.com/news/IRS-Tax-Preparer-Regulation-50697-1.html+tax+preparer+regulations+shulman+new+day&cd=10&hl=en&ct=clnk&gl=us&client=safari.

5. H&R Block, Inc. F1Q10 Earnings Call Transcript, September 4, 2009, http://webcache.googleusercontent.com/search?q=cache:N62JanV4jgwJ:seekingalpha.com/article/160035-h-amp-r-block-inc-f1q10-qtr-end-07-31-09-earnings-call-transcript+russ+smyth+three+keys+to+success&cd=1&hl=en&ct=clnk&gl=us&client=safari.

6. Alexander Eule, "Take Your Chips off H&R Block," *Barrons.com*, March 11, 2010, http://online.barrons.com/article_email/SB126831139841259835-lMyQ-jAxMTIwNjE4MTMxMTExWj.html.

7. Bill Carache, "H&R Block: Downgrading to Underperform on Execution Concerns," Macquarie (USA) Equities Research, February 22, 2010.

8. Joe DeLessio, "Opening Day at New Yankee Stadium a Bit Anticlimactic," *New York*, April 17, 2009, http://74.125.155.132/search?q=cache:NPPFfu56V8MJ:nymag.com/daily/intel/2009/04/opening_day_at_new_yankee_stad.html+new+yorker+h%26R+block+day+yankee+stadium&cd=5&hl=en&ct=clnk&gl=us&client=safari.

9. Peter Schwartz, "H&R Block Sponsorship at Yankee Stadium Needs An Audit," *Forbes.com*, April 14, 2010, http://blogs.forbes.com/sportsmoney/2010/04/sports-sponsorship-head-scratcher/.

10. Schedule 14(a), H&R Block, Inc. (Registrant), United States Securities and Exchange Commission, August 3, 2007, http://google.brand.edgar-online.com/DisplayFilingInfo.aspx?Type=HTML&text=%2526lt%253bNEAR%252f4%2526gt%253b(%22MARK%22%2C%22ERNST%22)&FilingID=5343165&ppu=%2FPeopleFilingResults.aspx%3FPersonID%3D3594888.

11. H&R Block Inc. F1Q09 Earnings Call Transcript, September 3, 2008, http://seekingalpha.com/article/93792-h-amp-r-block-inc-f1q09-qtr-end-7-31-09-earnings-call-transcript?page=-1&find=hrb.

12. Michael Millman, "H&R Block (HRB): Poor New Client Growth Hurts," Millman Research Associates, March 8, 2010.

Chapter Sixteen   A Taxing System

1. "Taxes: Taking Aim at a 'Disgrace,'" *Time*, July 4, 1977, www.time.com/time/magazine/article/0,9171,945778,00.html.

2. Ronald Reagan, "A Time for Choosing," October 27, 1964, http://74.125.155.132/search?q=cache:UvMnLOVB2PcJ:imkane.wordpress.com/mustreadingspeeches/+a+time+for+choosing+reagan+visitor+from+mars&cd=2&hl=en&ct=clnk&gl=us&client=safari.

3. Bob Weinstein, "Blockbuster," *Entrepreneur*, April 1992, 164.

Chapter Seventeen   Opening Doors

1. "UMKC Bloch School's Dean Tan means business," *Kansas City Business Journal*, September 4, 2009, http://74.125.155.132/search?q=cache:qmaUFqncmSAJ:kansascity.bizjournals.com/kansascity/stories/2009/09/07/editorial1.html+bloch+school+of+business&cd=25&hl=en&ct=clnk&gl=us&client=safari.

2. "Business School as Usual: Not for This Dean," *Bloch*, 2009, 3. *Bloch* is an annual journal "to encourage interest and support among alumni, partners and friends" and is published by the Henry W. Bloch School of Business and Public Administration.

3. Shirley Christian, "What's Doing in Kansas City?" *New York Times*, June 23, 2002, http://74.125.155.132/search?q=cache:iRR9oAYqeBEJ:www.nytimes .com/2002/06/23/travel/what-s-doing-in-kansas-city.html%3Fpartner%3D rssnyt%26emc%3Drss+henry+bloch+fountain&cd=18&hl=en&ct=clnk& gl=us&client=safari.

Chapter Eighteen Making an Impression

1. Leigh Christy, "Nelson-Atkins Museum of Art," *Architecture Week*, March 12, 2008, D1.2.

2. Toni Wood and Ann Slegman, *Bold Expansion: The Nelson-Atkins Museum of Art Bloch Building* (London: Scala, 2007), 5.

3. Rebecca Dimling and Bobbie Leigh, "100 Top Collectors Who Have Made a Difference," *Arts & Antiques*, March 2006, 90.

Chapter Nineteen And Then Some

1. Joyce Smith, "How to Succeed, and Then Some," *Kansas City Star*, 28 February, 2007, C2.

2. Gene Smith, "Bloch," *Topeka Capital Journal*, 11 January 1976, Sunday magazine section.

3. Justin Layhart, "An End to the Focus on Short Term Urged," *Wall Street Journal*, September 9, 2009, http://online.wsj.com/article/SB125244043531193463 .html.

Acknowledgments

T he creation of a book takes more than one person. I feel particularly indebted to Deborah Shouse, who edited these pages. I value her terrific talent and spot-on advice.

My agent, Jeff Herman, had an important part in bringing this book to life. He found a good home for it at John Wiley & Sons. Executive editor David Pugh and Senior Editorial Manager Emilie Herman took an immediate interest in the story and offered superb input and guidance. I hope this book is a source of pride to Deborah, Jeff, David, Emilie, and everyone who contributed to it in one form or another.

Many people were kind enough to provide information and spend time with me. I wish to express my special appreciation to the people I interviewed—Ken Baum, Alan Bennett, Annette Bloch, Leon Bloch Jr., Helen Bernstein Fealy, Fantashia Freeman, Barnett Helzberg, Charles Helzberg, John Helzberg, Joe Janco, Dustin Jensen, Bob Johnson, Dick Levin, Linda Lyon, Ed Matheny, Pat Merriman, David Miles, Jack Nachman, Jean Nachman, Jossy Nebenzahl, Miguel Pineda, Frank Psota, Bill Ross, Honey Scheidt, Elaine Sight, Russ Smyth, Michael Song, Morton Sosland, Teng-Kee Tan, Jim Thompson, Ken Treat,

Sr., Henry Wash, John White, and Marc Wilson. I also appreciate the help of Shaunda Parks at H&R Block, who assisted me in securing many of the photos in this book, and Todd Tedesco, senior production editor at John Wiley & Sons.

Special thanks to my dear wife, Mary, who cheerfully surrendered evenings and weekends while I tapped away at my keyboard. And as my first editor, she became nearly as familiar with Dad's story as I did. I am also indebted to my sons, Jason and Teddy, for their encouragement and support.

No statement of gratitude would be complete for a work such as this if I did not take account of the enormous help I received from my father, Henry Bloch. This book could not have been written without his help, his insight, and, most of all, his incredible journey. Giant thanks, Dad, for collaborating with me. I cherish the time we spent together.

The last obligation I must mention is my largest. It is to the people who make up H&R Block. They have generously given of themselves to serve our clients and support our mission. Thank you all.

About the Author

Thomas M. Bloch is an author, speaker, educator, entrepreneur, former CEO of H&R Block, and son of Henry Bloch.

Tom worked closely with his father at H&R Block for nearly two decades. Henry was Chairman of the Board when Tom was President and Chief Executive Officer. Their offices were next to each other. With the exception of Marion, his wife of 59 years, no one knows Henry Bloch better than Tom. This book benefits from their relationship.

Tom Bloch's career change in 1995 from CEO of H&R Block to inner-city teacher drew national media attention. Five years later, he cofounded the University Academy, an urban college preparatory charter school of 1,100 Kansas City students, where he taught middle school math and served as board president. Tom's highly acclaimed book, *Stand for the Best*, chronicles his journey from the corporate boardroom to an inner-city classroom.

Tom Bloch is Vice Chairman of the University of Missouri-Kansas City (UMKC) Trustees, and he is President of the Endowment Board of the Henry W. Bloch School of Business and Public Administration at UMKC. Tom is also a founding board member of the UMKC Foundation. He was a director of H&R Block from 1983 to 1995 and then from 2000 to 2010.

Tom and his wife, Mary, live in Kansas City, Missouri. They have two sons, Jason and Teddy.

Index

Index

Helzberg, Barnett, Sr., 44
Helzberg, Charles, 48, 195
Helzberg, Dr. John, 194–195
Helzberg, Horty, 54, 68, 70
Helzberg, Jim, 11, 47, 194
Helzberg, Marion. *See* Bloch,
    Marion Helzberg
Helzberg, Morton, 48, 50, 54
Helzberg Diamonds Shops, 44
Henry W. Bloch Fountain, at Union
    Station, 169–170
Henry W. Bloch Scholars Program,
    161–162, 165–169
Henry W. Bloch School of Business
    and Public Administration,
    162–165, 179–182
High Aspirations, 165
Hoffman, Carol, 49
Holl, Steven, 171
Hoover, Herbert, 5
H. O. Peet, 33–34
Hyatt, Joel, 112
Hyatt Legal Clinics, 112, 114

I

Institute for Entrepreneurship and
    Innovation (IEI), 163–165,
    179–182, 191–192
Insurance products, H&R Block's sale
    of, 101
Interim Services, 125
Internal Revenue Service. *See also*
    Tax code
    changes, electronic filing
        procedures, 125–126
    creation of, 151
    enrolled agents and, 84
    Ernst joins, 142
    first Form 1040, 151, 152
    Free File Alliance, 134
    investigations of fraudulent
        preparers, 100, 104

    plans to regulate tax preparation
        industry, 145
    stops preparing tax returns for free,
        65, 69
Ireland, 151

J

Jackson Hewitt, 135
Janco, Joe, 95, 97
Jensen, Justin, 165–166
Johnson, Bob, 80–83, 84, 91, 103

K

Kansas, Hospital of the University
    of, 131
Kansas City, University of, 8
Kansas City Country Club,
    121–124
Kansas City School of Law, 26
Kansas City Star, 60–62, 139
Kemp, Jack, 156

L

Leno, Jay, 150
Letterman, David, 137
Levin, Dick, 48, 49, 56
Liberty Tax Service, 135
Lincoln, Abraham, 28, 151
Long, Russell, 156
Long Island Newsday, 115–116
Louis, Joe, 19
Lucky Bastards Club, 18–19
Lyon, Linda Bloch (niece), 136

M

MacDill Air Base, Tampa Florida, 13
Mag, Arthur, 194
Mail Me Monday (MMM), 43
Matheny, Ed, 162, 196, 197
Mayo Clinic, 117
McGladrey & Pullen LLC, 128
McVoy, Chris, 172